simply ROSES

THE BRUMBACK LIBRARY

IN MEMORY OF:

Mr. John Miller

PRESENTED BY:

Mr. & Mrs. Charles Koch

all you need to know to grow beautiful roses

simply ROSES

the essential guide to easy gardening

Karen L. Dardick

Foreword by Tom Carruth

Introduction by Tommy Cairns

Photographs by Claire Curran

UNIVERSE

First published in the United States of America in 2003
by UNIVERSE PUBLISHING
A Division of Rizzoli International Publications, Inc.
300 Park Avenue South
New York, NY 10010
www.rizzoliusa.com

© 2003 by Karen L. Dardick
Photographs © by Claire Curran
Designed by Stephen Fay

All photographs are by Claire Curran, except for the following:
Courtesy of the American Rose Society: page 126
Gene Sasse, Courtesy of Weeks Roses: pages 115; ix (top left), xiii (top),
xv (top left and bottom)
Courtesy of Anthony Tesselaar: pages 65; ix (top right)

2003 2004 2005 2006 2007/ 10 9 8 7 6 5 4 3 2 1

Printed in Hong Kong

ISBN: 0-7893-1003-1

Library of Congress Control Number: 2003104954

contents

part one: getting started

part two: choosing your roses

part three: simple basics of rose gardening

part four: simple care

part five: rose potpourri

conclusion: enjoying your roses

acknowledgments

MY DEEP APPRECIATION GOES TO TOM CARRUTH, a talented and caring person who creates sensationally beautiful roses and also goes out of his way to share his vast knowledge.

My thanks go to Dorothy Reinhold. When she was features editor for the *Pasadena Star-News* and its related publications, she gave me the opportunity to write rose columns in which I could share my enthusiasm for the Queen of Flowers. When Catherine Gaugh assumed this position, she continued to support my endeavor.

To Bryce Martin, who shared many rosy experiences with me and helped change my black thumb to green. Many thanks to hybridizer Keith Zary, to rose expert Jacques Ferare, to landscape architect Shirley Kerins, to iris and daylily expert John Shoustra, to Dr. Tommy Cairns, and to my editor at Universe, Alex Tart, for her support and insightful comments.

Most especially, my love and appreciation to Bob Mason, whose unfailing support and incredible energy fill my life with rose petals of joy.

foreword

KAREN DARDICK HAS BEEN THROUGH ALL THE STAGES of rose love, from early infatuation and determined devotion to realistic rose rearing. As a garden writer, she's brought us along on all those stages of rose adoration. *Simply Roses* is a wonderful collection of those tales—a guidance through the many months of rose gardening and learning.

Roses have a bad rap. They often get targeted as prima donnas of the garden who require much more care and attention than other plants. In fear of their supposed "special" needs, gardeners often add insult to injury by isolating all their roses in a hideous geometric rose "bed" rather than letting them mingle with the "lower" level of complementary plants. But let's look at roses more realistically.

If you happen to drive by an old abandoned farmyard, you're quite likely to see a rose blooming away with virtually no pampering—struggling against all sorts of plant competition and fueled only by Mother Nature's occasional rain—proving its stamina as America's national flower. That's a far cry from what you might call mollycoddled. Yet if you think about how roses are sold in the nurseries, few plants can take being ripped out of the ground and stripped of all foliage to be shipped bare-root all over the country.

How many other perennials can give your garden as much of a performance as does a rose? It blooms all flowering season long, year after year, making your heart sing anew with each opening blossom. What may seem like an initial expense is returned to you multifold during the garden years to come.

Ironically, those of us who are possessed by the beauty of our Queen of Flowers (the rabid rosarians!) can easily belittle the average gardener with our zest about what is absolutely needed to pamper the rose properly. In our zeal to convert the nonbelievers, we end up intimidating the interested. But rose growing isn't really that complicated.

Truth is, there are hundreds—thousands—of rose varieties available, all with varying combinations of color, style, habit, fragrance, disease resistance, hardiness, usefulness, and panache. And, with a little guidance, it's very likely that you can find the rose that perfectly suits your personal needs, whatever those may be.

Simply Roses provides this guidance. May it help you to better understand and enjoy growing roses.

Tom Carruth
Director of Research, Weeks Roses

introduction

my life with roses

EVER SINCE I WAS A YOUNG BOY LIVING IN SCOTLAND with my parents, roses
have always been in my life. When adulthood arrived and I bought my first home in
Southern California it was perfectly natural, therefore, to incorporate roses into my
landscaping projects. Little did I know that those first dozen rose bushes would catapult me
into growing one thousand some five years later and that I would become president of the
American Rose Society, the largest horticultural society in the U.S., and vice president and
editor for the World Federation of Rose Societies.

I have often said that roses are in the blood. If you're like me, you're destined to love
and grow roses. At some point in your life the intensity for this hobby flourishes and you
embrace it with great passion. This devotion suddenly occupies your life, as I discovered
when one day I woke up a "rose evangelist." Attempting to dissect the reasons for this
change in my life has been futile, for I kept coming back to the basic fact that I love roses
and there's no doubt about it!

Joining the American Rose Society was the best step I took forward. What a terrific
society full of people just like myself! Soon I was flourishing in my newfound status as an
ARS consulting rosarian, using my educational background as a biochemist and chemist to
teach others the science behind rose growing. I took to exhibiting roses like the proverbial
fish to water! As a regular author for the ARS magazine I attracted the attention of key
leaders and was invited to chair various committees. I was selected to be editor for *Modern
Roses: The World Encyclopedia of Roses*, a position I have now held for the past twelve years.
A rose hybridizer named a rose in honor of my work, the elegant hybrid tea 'Editor Tommy
Cairns'. I started a local rose society in my hometown, aptly named the Tinseltown Rose
Society. In 2000, I became president of the American Rose Society. Almost twenty years
have passed since purchasing that first dozen rose bushes and I have thoroughly enjoyed the
interim crammed full of great memories and hundreds of new friends.

Looking back on these two decades of pleasure, it has been the roses and the people
that dominated my landscape. Roses provide a unique hobby that reinvents itself regularly.
Initially, you may grow roses for the simple pleasure of having the so-called Queen of
Flowers in your garden, relishing the beauty and fragrance for which they are known. Then

you may gravitate to exhibiting roses for the thrill of competition, first locally, then statewide, then nationally, and finally internationally! Joining the ARS promotes your volunteer spirit and soon you are an expert helping others. There is no finer pleasure for me than watching a novice grower become an expert, for I know the inner satisfaction of passing on my rose knowledge to others. Becoming a national officer in the American Rose Society is merely another extension of that deep-seated volunteer spirit.

And, if you're like me, the ultimate volunteer step is to get involved with the World Federation of Rose Societies. There is an old Scottish song by Harry Lauder that tells us to "keep right on to the end of the road." For rose growers there is no end to this road, for this is a hobby that has so many ramifications that intrigue and tempt the rose grower to meet the challenge of becoming one of the world's custodians of this very special flower.

Roses are easy to grow and their flowering gives an emotional high that pleases the senses as well as the mind. Abandon caution and accept the reckoning that can follow, for being a rose grower is a blessing as well as a calling! Join in and celebrate the rose and all the comforts it can bring to our hectic and complex lives.

Dr. Tommy Cairns

preface

metamorphosis of a former manhattanite

I'M AFFLICTED WITH A CONDITION CALLED ROSE FEVER. I burn with a desire to acquire, grow, and enjoy roses. The more, the better. At spring's onset, I wake up every morning with anticipation. Still clad in nightgown, robe, and slippers, before I've even had my morning tea, I rush outdoors to see what wonders await me in the garden. Have any more rosebuds formed? Are any fat buds swelling to reveal the tantalizing colors within? Are flowers unfurled enough to inhale sweet perfumes? If I see budworms—tiny green caterpillars that can devour rosebuds before they open, I remove the problems with my bare hands and crush them underfoot. If there are aphid colonies sucking sap from tender new canes, I strip them off before they can damage my cherished plants. I love my roses so much that I defend their health with vehemence.

I wasn't always like this. As a child growing up in the heart of New York, in Midtown Manhattan, I had nothing to do whatsoever with gardens. My parents decorated their luxurious apartment with antiques. My exposure to flowers was silk bouquets that never withered, still life paintings, or embellished decorative art. Our balcony was decorated with Astroturf that only needed an occasional hosing for cleaning. As I grew older, I became aware that I didn't like being in the country because it was overrun with insects. When I was eleven or twelve, my parents sent me to summer camp at East Hampton, where water sports were the major features. One of the first things I did upon arrival was phone my parents and frantically request a fly swatter so I could defend myself from flies, spiders, and other creepy-crawlers. Of course, they understood and immediately sent one.

I hated the idea of gardening at that point in my life because it would have meant putting my clean hands into dirt, which was disgustingly, well—dirty. As I grew into my teen years, I disdained any flower other than an orchid, which was worn as a shoulder or wrist corsage when I attended formal dances.

My metamorphosis occurred when I moved to Los Angeles in 1968. For the first time in my life, I saw trees covered in breathtaking flowers. I later learned they are jacaranda trees and I became enchanted by their delicate purple blossoms and feathery leaves. I also began to appreciate flower bouquets in my home, especially when the fragrance and appealing colors of roses brought living beauty indoors. I often bought roses to grace my living room. In 1983, I bought a house in Los Angeles. The simple California bungalow had enough space to plant a dozen rose bushes. I reasoned that it would be less expensive for me to grow my own rose bouquets than to purchase them from florists.

Time proved me wrong. I probably could have purchased an entire chain of florist stores for what I've spent on roses and related items during these past twenty or so years. When I planted those twelve bushes, they scarcely grew. So I joined a local rose society to learn how to grow roses. During these years I became afflicted with rose fever. As I came to understand what roses needed to grow well, I couldn't get enough of them. More and more varieties captured my interest. My garden quickly outgrew the space, so I did what any rose fancier would do. First came "diminishing lawn syndrome"—the removal of strips of lawn to accommodate more roses. But when the roses had swallowed the front and back lawns, I realized that I could solve my problem by selling the bungalow and buying a house with more land. So I did. Instead of sixty-five roses, I could grow hundreds of them. And I did. In the process, my journalism mixed with my love of roses. A new career as a garden writer emerged.

Growing, writing, and lecturing about roses occupied more and more of my time. In the process, I didn't really have time to fuss over each plant, to fertilize the bushes every week or two, or to apply chemicals that would fight off diseases and insects. My time constraints grew larger than my garden. I needed another way of gardening, a simpler way. I also came to the conclusion that a good deal of information about the care and nurturing of roses is disseminated by people who participate in rose shows. Their goals are to cultivate perfect flowers on long canes, with shiny, healthy leaves devoid of holes from hungry insects. My goals were less ambitious. I simply wanted roses to enjoy in the landscape, to bring indoors and to share with friends. I could be a little more forgiving if there were some flaws. As far as perfection of individual blossoms, I'm very forgiving, too. If the center is a little confused, if the form is other than an elegant, high shape with petals unfurling in perfect symmetry, that really doesn't disturb my enjoyment of the flower's essential beauty. I did once win a trophy at a local rose show when I decided to test my skills. With that accomplishment in hand, I preferred to spend my time writing about roses and sharing my enthusiasm and information. My aim is to simplify the rose growing process so it doesn't seem so overwhelming.

Planting a rose garden, or any garden for that matter, is an act of hope, faith, and courage. Hope that plants live and thrive, faith that the result goes according to plan, and courage to persevere despite harsh weather, insects, or diseases. It doesn't surprise me that according to national polls, gardening is America's number one outdoor leisure activity. (Bird watching is number two.) Nor does it surprise me that roses are the most popular of garden plants. For me, there's nothing like a rose. I love the diversity of flower shapes, colors, and forms. There are roses for almost every situation, from microminis to massive climbers. Roses can work as groundcover, to edge flower borders, or as the backbone of perennial gardens to ramble up trees or flank walls. Admittedly, roses sulk in shade. But given at least six hours of daily sunshine, their uses are limited only by one's imagination and pocketbook.

Perhaps you're hesitant to include roses in your landscape because of their reputation for taking too much work. Or, you might grow a few roses now and wonder why they don't thrive. But they really are easy to grow. Roses have existed on this planet for millions of years. Bushes can thrive at abandoned sites. They need comparatively little and return so much that they are well worth whatever time and effort you want to expend. I hope *Simply Roses* will enhance your enjoyment of rose gardening.

Karen L. Dardick

Yes, Roses Really Are Easy to Grow

"And Love's Own Flower the blushing Rose,
The Queen of all the garden close"
from Flora's Feast, A Masque of Flowers, by Walter Crane, 1889

I WISH I HAD A DOLLAR FOR EVERY TIME I've heard someone say, "Oh, I just love roses! But they're too hard to grow!" I reply that rose cultivation is as easy or as hard as one makes it.

My garden is filled with roses—climbing roses, hybrid tea roses, floribunda roses, tree roses, miniature roses, and a lot of the new David Austin English roses. I have well over one hundred, and like most people today, I don't have time to be a slave to my garden. It's there for my enjoyment, not my torture.

I want to spend at least several hours each week in my garden, tending to the roses while enjoying their dazzling colors, heady scents, and overall beauty reflected in my

landscape. But some weeks, I don't even have those few hours to spare.

When I first learned about growing roses, I joined a local rose society and received a great deal of advice from the experts on how to tend roses while striving to grow the perfect rose. And therein lies the mythology of troublesome roses. People who exhibit roses often follow rigorous schedules for fertilizing, spraying, pruning, and grooming their bushes in their efforts to capture blue ribbons and crystal trophies. This can often involve long hours in their gardens.

My efforts are less ambitious. Few perennial plants or shrubs provide as much color, as many blossoms, or as sweet a fragrance for so long a period of time in balmy Southern California as does the Queen of Flowers—the rose. I enjoy their beauty in the landscape or in their luscious bouquets that perfume the air. So, I can forgive the roses that have some holes in their leaves where hungry insects have chewed. I don't mind if the blossoms are not exhibition quality.

Therefore, tending them is much simpler. Start with the basics of selecting a sunny site, and make sure that the soil is fertile, well draining, and loaded with nutrients. You can do this by adding organic planting mix when planting, and mulching the top of the soil in spring or summer. You'll know that your soil is fertile and rich if earthworms have taken up residence.

Select roses with a hereditary resistance to the diseases that can attack them. Where I live, mildew and rust are the two culprits. In wetter climates, blackspot is the scourge. Many roses are naturally resistant to these, some are moderately so, and others are completely impervious to attack. You can locate them with a little research. Visit a public garden, ask a friend or neighbor, or consult some books. Local nurseries that carry a large supply of roses can also be good sources of information.

Once you've selected and planted your roses, ensure their health by regular fertilizing and watering. You don't have to overdo it—three or four feedings a year is all they need to thrive. Begin in early to late spring, depending on where you live, when the new growth is at least two inches long and leaves have formed. The simplest, but most expensive fertilizer is a small, coated, granular pellet that slowly releases nutrients to the soil over six to nine months, depending on the formula you select.

I prefer to save money and spend more time with my plants, so I use several different methods. When I prune in January I clean up the old leaves around each plant and scatter several handfuls of ground alfalfa meal. This is a source of nitrogen and hormones that aids the first flush of growth. I follow it up in March with a handful of all-purpose rose fertilizer per bush. Then, when the growth has developed a little more, I use liquid kelp as a foliar fertilizer.

After the first bloom cycle ends, apply another round of fertilizer, either by scattering granular fertilizer around the base, or using a liquid applied to the leaves. Stop in summer, when high heat is already stressing the roses. In warm climates, feed once more in mid-September and you'll be rewarded with December roses.

I haven't sprayed my roses for pests or diseases for years, and the roses are thriving. Yes, aphids attack roses, especially in spring when succulent new growth attracts them. I resort to hosing them off, releasing ladybugs, lacewings, and other predatory "good" bugs, and letting nature handle the rest.

Other than winter pruning, during most of the year, the most time-consuming task is cutting the blossoms for indoor display or deadheading the plants when the blooms are finished. This is one of my favorite pastimes. I also love to stroll through my garden on a languid late afternoon, cup of tea in one hand, the other outstretched to caress a particularly lovely bloom.

I confess that I will find other tasks to do in my garden when I particularly want to pamper my roses, but that's more to satisfy my need to nourish them than it is for their own requirement. After all, roses are often left neglected and untended in abandoned farms or centuries-old cemeteries, and they flourish. The Queen of Flowers is really a very tough plant.

Roses Come in
Many Forms

T HAT DOESN'T LOOK LIKE A ROSE" is the typical response of a person seeing any other type of rose besides a hybrid tea for the first time. But in fact, the flower form that most people think of as a rose is a newcomer in the venerable history of the rose's development. That elegant, high-centered hybrid tea rose cloaked in many petals came into being in 1867, when 'La France', the first hybrid tea rose, was introduced. It became the demarcation between modern roses and Old Garden Roses. Since then, hybrid tea roses have dominated the rose marketplace for more than a hundred years, and have become the tokens of love and esteem that florists deliver on Valentine's or Mother's Day.

In nature, all roses began with a simple five-petaled shape which botanists have termed "single." These wild, original roses are called species roses. All roses, ancient and modern, are descendents and share the heritage of a single flower form. Species roses are ancient. Fossil remains date back at least thirty-two million years. And during these aeons, people of many cultures have cultivated and enjoyed the rose in many different ways. Flower shapes changed in part due to selection of species that naturally mutated and had more petals, and in great part due to the efforts of rose breeders who wanted to create roses with more petals and a variety of forms and shapes.

Roses are not the only flowers that have many different types of flower forms. Chrysanthemums, camellias, and dahlias are examples of hybridizers creating multiple types of flower with specific designations and descriptions.

Rose forms are classified by just a few terms:

Single—the flower has just five petals, such as species or wild roses or 'Starry Night', a modern shrub

Semi-double—the flower has six to sixteen petals, such as 'Playboy' or Blueberry Hill'

Double—the flower has seventeen to twenty-five petals, such as 'Bride's Dream', 'Iceberg', and 'Hot Cocoa'

Full—the flower has twenty-six to forty petals, such as 'Top Notch', 'Proud Land', and 'Mister Lincoln'

Very full—the flower has forty-one or more petals, such as 'Peace', 'Seashell', or 'Toro'

SINGLE

SEMI-DOUBLE

DOUBLE

FULL

VERY FULL

These descriptions are defined by the American Rose Society and people who breed roses. From these few forms spring thousands of varieties of modern and antique roses. Flower forms vary so greatly that many people don't recognize them as roses. Standards of beauty also change over time. With the popularity of the David Austin English roses has come an appreciation of rose shapes that differ greatly from the hybrid tea form. In response, hybridizers are introducing roses with fewer petals that are old-fashioned in appearance such as flat, cupped, or quartered, reminiscent of Old Garden Roses.

'Fourth of July' is an example of a recent rose introduction that looks very different from typical florist roses. It was created by Altadena resident Tom Carruth, who directs the rose breeding program at Weeks Roses in Upland, California. Winner of the coveted All-America Rose Selections (AARS) award in 1999, each brilliantly colored flower on 'Fourth of July' consists of just five petals, a form that wasn't very popular just a few years ago. Because the rose-buying public is becoming interested in flower forms besides hybrid teas, rose breeders are responding. Carruth estimates that of the more than thirty rose varieties he's developed, almost half are singles and semi-doubles.

The interest in old-fashioned forms is encouraging other breeders to create more. The choices are greater now than ever before. No matter which form of flower you prefer, you can be assured that a rose is a rose is a rose, even if it doesn't look like it.

What Type of Rose Is Best?

THE LATE GERTRUDE STEIN penned the immortal phrase "a rose is a rose is a rose," but she didn't take into account that there are at least one hundred species of roses. There may even be two hundred, if botanists can agree on their characteristics.

Gardeners who want to include roses in their landscapes face a daunting task of selecting just a few from the thousands of varieties commercially available. Although most nurseries stock from fifty to five hundred, the choices increase if you seek out mail-order rose companies that offer even more.

You can simplify your choices by considering the growth and blooming habits that rose experts and hybridizers use to categorize roses. The first is the distinction between antique and modern roses. Before 1867, there were only what we now call antique roses—species of wild or cultivated roses classified as follows: alba, Bourbon, centifolia, China, damask, gallica, moss, polyantha, Portland, tea, hybrid perpetual, rambler, and climber. (See pages 53–55 for detailed descriptions.) Many are still grown today by fanciers who love their forms and fragrances.

Since the first hybrid tea rose, 'La France', emerged in 1867, tens of thousands of hybrid tea varieties have been created, as well as floribundas, grandifloras, miniatures, modern climbers, and shrubs. Hybrid teas have almost become synonymous with the word "rose." They are characterized as roses that produce one bloom per stem and usually grow from three to five feet tall. In the early 1920s, as gardeners clamored for plants to fit into smaller spaces, came the introduction of floribunda roses, compact plants with clusters of blooms on shorter stems. The rose revolution continued with the introduction in 1954 of 'Queen Elizabeth', the first grandiflora rose—a taller plant, growing up to six feet, with both single blooms and clusters at the end of the majestic canes.

I recently moved and planted a new garden from scratch. I can't bear to be without climbing roses because these are the workhorses of the landscape. So, I installed a long, freestanding wrought iron fence to support them and planted six lovely climbers. A rose like 'Sally Holmes', which spans twenty feet, is guaranteed to produce an astronomic quantity of flowers. But so much beauty comes at a price. Climbers are the most labor intensive, especially during winter when it's time for their annual pruning.

I also love hybrid tea roses for their elegant stems and flower form. I adorn my house with vases filled with their stunningly beautiful blossoms. Miniature roses are useful to tuck in the front of the border or in containers to highlight sunny decks or patios. Many varieties are fragrant as well as cheerfully colorful. The easiest of all to tend are the new varieties of shrub roses. These are rose bushes that produce masses of colorful blossoms that usually don't have the classic hybrid tea form. Most also lack fragrance. They make up for those shortcomings by producing lots of color on plants that are virtually disease-free so they take little tending.

An estimated thirty thousand species and cultivars of roses are available, although you'd have to search long and hard for some.

Antique or
Modern Roses
what's the difference?

WHAT'S OLD IS SUDDENLY NEW, at least for many rose lovers. Flower forms and styles that had flourished many centuries ago are getting a rebirth in contemporary rose gardens. People who had disdained anything but the tapered, high-centered hybrid tea, the darling of florists, are taking another look at what the rose kingdom has to offer.

The dowagers who once reigned in many a rose garden over the centuries until twentieth-century rose hobbyists regarded them as dumpy and déclassé are enjoying a resurgence of appreciation for their fragrance, romance, and cupped, ruffled, or quartered flower forms. A debate now rages among adherents of Old Garden Roses and admirers of modern roses.

What is an Old Garden Rose? The official term doesn't refer to any rose discovered in a neglected garden. The American Rose Society classifies Old Garden Roses (more conveniently referred to as OGRs) as any roses introduced before 1867. That year is considered the boundary line between old and modern, at least as far the rose world is concerned, because it was the year of the introduction of a remarkable rose named 'La France', the very first hybrid tea rose. It was the start of a highly prized characteristic in roses—high-centered blossoms that repeated throughout the gardening year.

Roses have been flourishing on the planet even longer than humans. Fossil evidence in

Oregon and Colorado reveals that rose blossoms beautified the earth at least thirty-two million years ago. In addition to North America, they grew in Europe, the Middle East, and Asia. While experts can't determine exactly when humans began cultivating and breeding roses, they do have evidence that roses graced gardens in China approximately five thousand years ago. Ancient Egyptians placed rose wreaths in the tombs of their dead. Greeks and Romans used roses for ceremonies, festivals, and ornamentation. By the Middle Ages, roses were as valued for medicinal purposes as they were for their beauty.

But European roses, although hardy to the cold weather, bloomed just once a year, each spring. In the early 1800s, roses cultivated in China were brought into Europe. These remarkable roses had the ability to rebloom throughout the summer, a term called remontance. Some of them also bloomed in yellow and orange, colors not previously seen in European roses. Hybridizers eagerly experimented with these new rose varieties and worked to combine the best of all traits in new roses. At last, in 1867, a new classification was created when 'La France' was born.

During the past century, rose lovers have been able to choose among a seemingly bewildering number of varieties, with vocal advocates extolling the charms of OGR families of gallica, damask, centifolia, moss, Portland, China, noisette, tea, Bourbon, and hybrid perpetual roses. Equally vociferous are the admirers of modern hybrid tea, floribunda, grandiflora, miniature, or shrub roses.

Some generalizations can help buyers decide. For the most part, OGRs tend to sprawl, arch, spill, or ramble. They can grow into very large shrubs rather than bushes. They also produce roses on short stems, in comparison with modern roses, and the blooms can be short-lived, lasting just a few days. But the admirers are quick to point out their showy displays, intense fragrance, and charming flower form.

Lovers of modern roses admire their beautiful, high-centered buds, stem lengths, and range of colors. Modern roses also tend to be more resistant to fungal diseases. On the downside, fragrance has been sacrificed to disease-resistance.

My personal way of resolving this dilemma is to grow modern roses that have fragrance plus an inherent disease resistance. For old-fashioned flower charm, I include David Austin English roses, Romantica roses, and other new shrubs that combine the forms of OGRs with the more desirable repeat-bloom trait of modern roses. I think I have the best of the old and the new.

How to Choose Roses from Catalogues

I LOVE READING ROSE CATALOGUES. I read each from cover to cover, lingering over roses that are new introductions, and plan how to include yet more varieties into a rapidly filling garden. Years of reading and buying from catalogues have helped me realize some useful tips when shopping from a catalogue or a Web site.

First, it helps to have a little healthy skepticism. No matter whose catalogue you read, it seems that each and every rose variety is the very best. Remember, it's the company's job to sell roses, and their copywriters are skilled at putting positive spins on each and every variety. Personally, I have rarely met a rose I didn't like, and I'm ready to forgive many faults. But I do want a rose that blooms a lot, has at least moderate fragrance, and good disease resistance.

Most catalogues do a good job describing disease resistance for each variety, but if it isn't mentioned, beware. The plant may be susceptible to mildew, rust, or blackspot. Unless your heart is absolutely set on that particular rose, you may want to select a similar color and shape with better disease resistance.

When it comes to fragrance, it takes careful reading to determine which roses will have nose allure. Beware of any variety described as mild or light. What little scent there is won't be discerned in a hot climate and may be faint elsewhere. When reading descriptions, look for adjectives such as "heavy" or "strong." Also, beware of such descriptive phrases as "smells like bread dough" or "smells like Granny Smith apples." The fragrance may be so subtle that you can miss it altogether. To be fair, some roses have a very strong aroma in humid climates, but little where it's hot and dry. Be sure to select varieties clearly described as strongly fragrant.

Catalogues are visual enticements. Keep that in mind when you look over the photographs. It's a safe generalization that a rose in the garden rarely looks like its depiction in the catalogue. Only perfect blooms are selected for modeling, and they are highlighted, groomed, and lit in a way a garden rose never is. Also, catalogue photos rarely show the entire plant, so you can't judge a rose bush's garden performance by a single depiction.

Now for the fun of trying to judge its height and placement in your own garden. Keep in mind that these catalogues are written for a national market, and in much of the nation, the growing season varies. This means that a rose that's listed as three or four feet tall can grow to six or seven feet in the west or southwest where sunshine almost never ends. For example, 'Sally Holmes' is a well-behaved floribunda on the East Coast, and in my garden is a climbing rose with gargantuan proportions of twenty feet. The same thing happens when European roses reach California, as we discovered with the David Austin English roses that explode in California sunshine. Some catalogue descriptions try to give geographic variations.

In general, it's wise to see a rose variety growing in a local garden before deciding if you want that same one in your own garden. That sage advice is rarely followed, because catalogues arrive at a time when rose bushes are going dormant or are soon to be pruned. Prudent people wait until spring or summer, then study their chosen varieties in public or private gardens. I rarely have the patience and instead place my order the day I receive the catalogue. Sometimes it's a happy selection, but other years I replace a disappointment with something even more enticing.

Whether you buy from a catalogue or a store, be fair to the new rose and give it at least a three-year evaluation. It takes a year or two for a rose to root strongly and become at home in a garden's unique microclimate. What may seem to be a variety with stingy blooms in its first year or two can turn into a rose factory in subsequent years. Or, it may remain a disappointment and a candidate for replacement in the future.

Some catalogues are really informative about how to grow roses and can remain in your rose library for years. Among my favorites are Edmunds Roses, beloved by rose exhibitors, and Heirloom Old Garden Roses, which offers a large selection of Old Garden Roses and some modern varieties.

In Victorian England, pink roses meant grace and beauty; a deep red rose meant bashful shame; a purple rose meant sorrow; and a yellow rose symbolized jealousy or secrecy.

Red Roses

EVERY HOLIDAY SEASON, I decorate my house with festive flowers and foliage. I'm very sentimental and enjoy using the traditional color patterns of red and green. Garlands of holly, with bright red berries, red poinsettias, and red amaryllis bring warmth and cheer and memories of past Christmas celebrations. I especially enjoy harvesting the last roses of the season, and rejoice that the warm Southern California climate permits this when rose beds in most of the nation are slumbering under winter snow.

Red roses are especially welcome at this time of year. If you don't have any, or want to add more, this is also a good time to assess your rose collection and plan to buy new ones in the coming year.

Red remains the most popular of all the rose colors, both for gift-giving and home landscape use. When I decide to add a new rose variety to my garden, I look for one that is disease-free, flowers freely, has fragrance, produces beautifully shaped flowers, and is a plant with an attractive overall shape. Then I'm faced with reality because this perfect rose doesn't exist. Every variety has some flaw. It may smell sweet but get covered with mildew. Flowers may be knockouts but appear just a few at a time. Or maybe the shrub is so ungainly that you want to hide it from sight.

Then there's the color. Red may fade to purple-red. Or red might just have too much orange. Varieties are described as cherry red, scarlet red, black red, and so on.

There are even more choices if you consider rose categories, ranging from tiny miniature shrubs to tall climbers. In between are red hybrid tea roses, grandifloras, shrubs, floribundas, and shrublets, a new class from Weeks Roses for bushes that are larger than miniatures and smaller than floribundas.

So in deciding which new red roses belong in a garden, first consider the room in which they can grow. Then decide if fragrance is more important than appearance. Some of the most popular red rose varieties are likely to get mildew and may take a little extra care, but their perfume may be enticing. A number of red roses have eye appeal but don't tantalize the nose. If only we could have it all!

Some old favorites remain popular sellers, even though they're competing with dozens of new varieties. 'Mister Lincoln' and 'Chrysler Imperial' are both hybrid tea roses that are standing the test of time. Both are heavenly fragrant, but as flowers age, they lose their deep red hue and turn bluish purple. 'Europeana' is a low-growing floribunda that has been popular for decades. Its problems are lack of fragrance and strong tendency to mildew.

One of the world's most popular roses is the intense red hybrid tea 'Ingrid Bergman', a lovely variety, but sadly lacking in fragrance. When 'Olympiad' was introduced in 1984, it was reputed to be the best red rose on the market. That's true in terms of color, flower form, disease resistance, and profusion of bloom, but sadly, 'Olympiad' has no fragrance.

I'm crazy about 'Scentimental', a heavily perfumed red and white striped rose that is wonderfully impervious to disease. To me, its only flaw is that flowers last just a few days. However, the bush flowers frequently, so this is a flaw I can live with.

Some new varieties are heavily perfumed and can be worthy of a spot in your garden if you like the old-fashioned flower forms of antique roses on modern shrubs.

'Francois Rabelais' and 'Traviata' are two of the new Romantica series of roses that offer true red flowers on compact plants. They are both somewhat fragrant and have good disease resistance.

Other notable red varieties are:

'Black Magic'—This florist rose can be grown in gardens, too. It's so red it looks black.

'Crimson Bouquet'—This grandiflora grows medium to tall, with bright red flowers and a slight fragrance.

'Dolly Parton'—It has big, bold orange-red flowers and is very fragrant.

'Isabelle Renaissance'—Wonderful fragrance characterizes this tall shrub with old-fashioned flowers and good disease resistance.

'Lavaglut'—In German, the name means "lava glow," an apt description of the dark red flower clusters.

'Opening Night'—An offspring of 'Olympiad', this true red rose also has shapely flowers and good disease resistance, but little fragrance.

'Raven'—An offspring of 'Lavaglut', this small shrub produces quantities of dark red, velvety flowers with good form, good disease resistance, but little fragrance. Grows best in dry climates.

'Salsa'—This low-growing floribunda has bright red flowers, set off by showy yellow stamens. It has strong disease resistance, but slight fragrance.

'Showbiz'—The compact, rounded growth of this floribunda contributes to its popularity. Fire-engine red flowers are produced in profuse clusters. Disease resistance is excellent, but fragrance is scarce.

'Veterans' Honor'—Many rose experts regard this rose named to honor the men and women who have served in America's armed forces as among the best red hybrid tea roses to date. Bright red, high-centered flowers last a long time in a vase or on the bush. Plant is very disease-resistant. If it only had fragrance, it would be near perfect.

Yellow Roses
that shine in the garden

YELLOW FLOWERS in the landscape add a bright touch to any garden, and that's certainly true with yellow roses. Either planted in a group, or combined with blue, purple, lavender, or pink flowers, yellow roses belong in every garden.

Gardeners in the hot regions have to select their varieties with care because these sunshine roses don't always stay that way in the fierce, hot rays of the sun. Unfortunately, some of the most striking varieties fade out until the blossoms are almost white.

That was my experience with a lovely variety, 'Gold Medal', introduced in 1982. A tall grandiflora, 'Gold Medal' has many virtues, but color longevity isn't one of them. The best way to enjoy this variety is to pick the flowers in tight bud, and watch them unfurl in all their golden splendor indoors.

Yellow roses also have another undesirable characteristic—many are very disease-prone. We can thank *Rosa foetida persiana* ('Persian Yellow') for this. This old species is the ancestor of our modern yellow roses, and unfortunately, 'Persian Yellow' is extremely prone to blackspot.

Except for a few types of species roses, heritage roses don't come in yellow. Hybridizers determined to change that, and in the process, used 'Persian Yellow' as a parent. In 1900, Joseph Pernet-Ducher crossed it with a hybrid perpetual rose to create the first modern yellow variety, 'Soleil d'Or', a smash hit in its native France. It wasn't until 'Soleil d'Or' was grown in other countries that rose fanciers learned that blackspot was a recurring problem with 'Soleil d'Or' and subsequent yellow varieties. This disease, plus a general lack of vigor in yellow roses, are some of the reasons why it's so hard to create outstanding yellow varieties with strong, clear color, flower form, disease resistance, good growth habits, hardiness, and fragrance.

Fortunately, some clever breeders have succeeded in bringing to the market really garden-worthy yellow varieties in the major rose classifications of hybrid tea, floribunda, grandiflora, and shrub. The following are some of my favorites:

'Baby Love'—a Shrublet by Weeks Roses; butter yellow single flowers appear on a two-foot plant. Grow it among lavender or blue flowering plants for visual excitement.

'Brite Lites'—floribunda that is almost always in flower with clear yellow blooms.

'Celebrity'—a lovely hybrid tea with long-lasting flowers, excellent in bouquets or landscapes.

'Golden Celebration'—The David Austin English roses have caught on in California, but these imported beauties can grow so vigorously in this land of perennial sunshine that they outgrow their garden space. That's the problem with a lovely Austin variety, 'Graham Thomas', which can soar up to fourteen feet in hot climates, although in colder regions is a very manageable shrub. 'Golden Celebration' is a welcome alternative because it offers vibrant yellow, honey-sweet blooms with old-fashioned form, but on a smaller plant that can stretch to seven feet.

'King's Ransom'—An award-winning AARS hybrid tea in 1962, this was the most popular yellow rose for two decades. It's still a royal ruler in the yellow rose division with high pointed buds that open into blooms with fruity fragrance.

'Midas Touch'—vivid yellow hybrid tea that really loves heat. Most yellow roses aren't fragrant, but this one offers a mild musk aroma. Plant is disease-resistant and flowers are long-lasting.

'St. Patrick'—This novel yellow rose is tinged with green and thrives in heat. As temperatures increase, so does the greenish color in the long-lasting flowers.

'Summer Sunshine'—A hybrid tea that is one of the first to bloom in spring, this rose has been around since 1962. The cheerful yellow flowers have a mild fragrance.

'Sunsprite'—This floribunda is the only yellow rose among the world's top ten roses. Tom Carruth calls this a fantastic variety because of its deep lasting yellow color, disease resistance, and strong, sweet licorice fragrance.

In ancient Rome, a yellow rose suspended from the ceiling of a banqueting hall meant that everything said in that room had to be kept secret.

Think Pink

PINK IS A COLOR, a common term for dianthus, and a word meaning "the highest degree" as "he's in the pink of health." It's no wonder then that pink roses are among the most beloved and popular of these fabulous flowers. Ranging from soft, shimmery pink to bold, startling magenta, roses can be obtained in many different shades of pink. From the earliest species roses such as *Rosa carolina* and *Rosa palustris* to the present 'Timeless', a recent AARS winner, pink roses have attracted the attention of rose lovers from time immemorial.

In my own garden, I have more than forty varieties of pink roses, ranging from the miniature 'Cupcake' to the soaring climber 'Claire Rose'. In between, I've selected 'Tiffany', 'Mary Rose', 'Bewitched', 'Fragrant Memory', 'Bride's Dream', and 'Secret'—a white blushed with a pink that intensifies as the flowers age.

I'm also captivated by 'Sexy Rexy', a floribunda rose that produces masses of hot pink flowers with ruffled edges, as well as the very thorny hybrid tea, 'Pristine', which is white heavily blushed with pink. Some of the roses I include in my garden are well known and have been grown for decades—'Bewitched' and 'Tiffany'. Others are newcomers and have not yet caught on with the gardening public, like 'Queen Margrethe', a pale pink compact shrub with old-fashioned, quartered flowers, and fresh-cut-apple fragrance.

I favor pink and pink blends because they harmonize with so many colors, both indoors and out. Pink roses combine well with flowers of white, lavender, red, and even yellow hues.

In the language of flowers, pink conveys definite sentiments. Light pink means admiration or sympathy. Dark pink is gratitude or appreciation.

The best-selling rose in America, in terms of sheer volume, is Flower Carpet available in pink and apple blossom. It is followed by pink 'Simplicity', marketed by Jackson & Perkins as a living fence. The initial offering was pink, and over time, white, red, and yellow 'Simplicity' have been created. Easy to grow, and popular in many gardens, 'Simplicity' has masses of flowers and light green foliage that is completely disease-resistant. The pink flowers do spot if wetted by rain or heavy watering.

A pink rose made history in the 1950s when famed hybridizer Dr. Walter Lammerts created a rose so different that it didn't fit into any existing category. He named his majestic new rose 'Queen Elizabeth', and it truly was in a class all its own. Taller than hybrid tea plants, it produces one rose per stem like a hybrid tea, as well as clusters of flowers, like a floribunda. The All-America Rose Selections (AARS), the organization that governs roses, created a special category for it, grandiflora. This variety is still very popular with gardeners.

Another pink rose, 'Bonica', also made history when AARS had to create a new category for it. 'Bonica' was the first of the explosive new class of shrub roses. Masses of color in a garden on a large ball of very disease-resistant plant, 'Bonica' made a sensation when it appeared commercially in 1987.

You can find pink roses in just about any size plant, modern or antique.

These are some of my other favorite pink roses:

'Bride's Dream'—This hybrid tea is a long-stemmed variety originally created for the florist industry. High-pointed buds gradually open into pale pink, long-lasting flowers. There's good disease resistance but little fragrance.

'Cape Cod'—This excellent groundcover is strongly disease-resistant and blooms freely from spring to fall. Flowers are single form and are produced in numerous quantities. The honey fragrance attracts bees.

'Diana, Princess of Wales'—This pink blend hybrid tea, bred by Keith Zary for Jackson & Perkins and released in 1988, offers high-centered, sweetly fragrant flowers on a vigorous plant that has very good disease resistance.

'Flower Carpet Pink'—An excellent plant for a landscape or large container, it is virtually disease-resistant and produces huge clusters of deep pink flowers. The plant is low-growing and spreads four to five feet in three to four years.

'Gene Boerner'—A floribunda named in honor of a great rose hybridizer, this is a vigorous plant with excellent disease resistance. Slightly spicy, pure pink flowers in clusters are long-lasting on the plant, which grows upright.

'Mary Rose'—This is one of my favorite Austin roses because of the damask fragrance wafting from the medium pink flowers and because of the overall good disease resistance of the plant. In warm climates, this variety grows six or seven feet tall and wide. In regions of frost, the size is usually three to four feet.

'Secret'—Fragrance, beautiful flowers, and a plant that's easy to grow—I couldn't ask for more from a hybrid tea that produces loads of creamy flowers edged with rich pink and a strong, spicy scent.

'New Zealand'—This light pink hybrid tea has luscious fragrance, classic high-centered flowers, and amazing disease resistance. The plant grows upright, from four to six feet.

'Pretty Jessica'—Here's another Austin English rose that I cherish because it stays small so it's suited to small urban gardens or containers. Pale pink flowers have old-fashioned charm and sweet honey fragrance. The plant may get some mildew or rust.

'Queen Elizabeth'—The original grandiflora is still one of the best. It deserves world-wide popularity because of the profusion of medium pink flowers that adorn the stately bush that grows from six to ten feet tall.

Striped Roses

Striped roses are causing quite a sensation in the rose world, from tall climbing roses to tiny miniature blooms. Stripes in roses aren't new. The world's oldest happened by chance when a sport (spontaneous mutation) appeared on the ancient Rosa Gallica Officinalis, better known as the Apothecary Rose. Named 'Rosa Mundi', it still can be found growing in gardens around the world.

Ten Carefree Roses

I'M A GREEDY GARDENER, especially when it comes to roses. I want lots of rose blossoms, and I like it even better when the rose bushes require little of me other than routine watering, fertilizing, and some pruning. I go out of my way to select carefree roses for my urban garden. Because I spend so much time writing about roses and other flowers, I can't pamper fussy prima donnas who demand special care.

That means I'm often experimenting. Those that don't fulfill my requirements don't remain in my garden. My roses have to be disease-free because I begrudge the time or effort to spray them against the common rose fungi that can plague my region—downy mildew, powdery mildew, or rust.

I also avoid spraying even the non-toxic fungicides or insecticides because: a) I'd rather spend my time smelling the roses; b) my cats love to lounge beneath the bushes and I don't want to disturb them; c) I don't want to hassle the multitudes of bees, spiders, ladybugs, green lacewings, and other good bugs battling the hostile hordes of invading bad bugs.

I prefer carefree roses and am grateful to the rose hybridizers who have worked hard to create roses with excellent disease resistance. I do have some labor-intensive roses in my garden—some climbing roses and about a half-dozen David Austin English roses. I don't include these in my carefree category because even though I'm selective about their disease resistance, these rambunctious plants require considerable staking and pruning.

For people who want an easy rose garden consisting of roses for cutting and roses for garden enjoyment, I recommend the following: 'Bonica', 'Dream Orange', 'Carefree Delight', 'Duet', 'French Lace', 'Iceberg', 'Olympiad', 'Regensberg', 'Scentimental', and 'Secret'. These are a nice mixture of shrub roses, floribunda roses, and hybrid tea roses.

Both 'Scentimental' and 'Secret' are at the top of my list and belong in every garden.

They are both highly fragrant and almost completely free of disease. I love the bold stripes of 'Scentimental' and its spicy fragrance. I also appreciate the demure beauty of 'Secret'. Another admirable rose is the old standby, 'Duet', a workhorse of a rose that produces bouquets of hot pink flowers with ruffled edges. Alas, though, she has scant fragrance. Nor does 'Olympiad' perfume the air. But this clear red hybrid tea is so vigorous and produces so many flowers that I forgive the lack of scent.

'Bonica' is excellent in a landscape where it forms a round mass of color. 'Carefree Delight' is another excellent shrub. It was an AARS winner in 1996 and is almost always covered with single pink flowers with a white eye. 'Regensberg' is a floribunda rose that packs a lot of color in a small space, and looks like a small round ball of color when in flower, which is much of the year.

'Iceberg' is often called one of the world's ten great roses. Consistently beautiful with heavy masses of white flowers, it's excellent in the landscape and in bouquets.

For people who want an easy rose garden, consisting of roses for cutting and roses for garden enjoyment, I recommend the following:

'Scentimental'—This award-winning (AARS) floribunda boasts strongly fragrant flowers displaying bold stripes of burgundy red swirled with cream. No two flowers are alike. The plant is vigorous and can grow to five feet in warm climates.

'Secret'—This demure rose is white with a pink blush on the edges. A fragrant hybrid tea AARS winner, it is always attractive, super fragrant, and very simple to grow.

'Duet'—A workhorse of a rose, Duet produces bouquets of hot pink flowers with ruffled edges but has scant fragrance.

'Olympiad'—Although it doesn't perfume the air, this clear red hybrid tea is so vigorous and produces so many flowers that I can forgive the lack of scent.

'Bonica'—The first landscape shrub rose to win the coveted AARS award (1987), it is excellent in a landscape where it forms a round mass of color.

'Carefree Delight'—Another excellent shrub, it was an AARS winner in 1996 and is almost always covered with pink single flowers with a white eye.

'Regensberg'—A floribunda rose that packs a lot of color in a small space, Regensberg looks like a small round ball of color when in flower, which it is much of the year. It has little fragrance but lots of charm and great disease resistance.

'Iceberg'—One of the world's great roses, it has large masses of white flowers, which look beautiful in the landscape.

'Simplicity'—The name says it all. This floribunda was bred and marketed as a living fence because it's easy to grow, doesn't require deadheading, and looks great in mass plantings. The first variety was pink, and now there are more colors from which to choose.

'Betty Boop'—This is a real doll of a plant because the floribunda just keeps flowering and flowering and flowering. No need to remove spent blooms—the plant does it for you. Vivid colors of yellow edged with bright red fade to white edged with deep red.

'Dream Orange'—This floribunda has excellent disease resistance and nonstop flowering.

Ten Roses to Reconsider

THERE'S RARELY A ROSE THAT I DON'T LIKE. Just about every rose variety offered for sale is worthy of a place in someone's garden, somewhere. It's just too expensive for breeders and rose specialists to produce rose varieties that don't make the grade.

But every once in a while, I've grown a rose that hasn't met my expectations. Or sometimes it's a case of the wrong rose in the wrong space. Then, too, over the decades, good varieties are surpassed with new, improved versions. With so many excellent varieties from which to choose, why settle for a rose with inherent problems or lackluster performance?

Here are ten to avoid if you want easy-care roses:

'Alba Meidiland'—One of the first roses developed as a groundcover, it is now surpassed by better versions that bloom longer and more often. Instead, try 'White Meidiland' or 'Pearl Meidiland'.

'Betty Prior'—This venerable floribunda is prized for delicate single flowers. However, the plant attracts mildew, especially in western regions, like moths to flames. If you like single flowers, choose some of the great new varieties like 'Playboy' or 'Playgirl'.

'Brandy'—Prized by many for warm apricot, classically formed hybrid tea flowers, this plant needs a lot of pampering for survival in cold climates. Then there are the thorns—one plant can pack a nasty wallop to unsuspecting children or pets. Better choices include 'Just Joey' or 'Chris Evert'.

'Cl. Blaze'—This used to be the best climbing red rose available. Now, 'Cl. Altissimo' or 'Cl. Don Juan' provide more flower power.

'Cl. Dortmund'—This vigorous climbing rose has gorgeous red flowers and looks great on large fences or stone walls. However, its thorns should be classified as lethal weapons because they curve like fishhooks and pierce flesh unmercifully. Once, when I pruned this plant, I had so many gashes that friends inquired if I'd been in an accident.

'Cl. Golden Showers'—This fragrant climbing rose was a winner when it was introduced in 1956. However, the yellow flowers fade in summer sun. Instead, consider 'Cl. Flutterbye' or 'Cl. Autumn Sunset'.

'John F. Kennedy'—The memory of this great American president for whom the hybrid tea is named keeps it a sentimental favorite. But there are many more garden-worthy white roses from which to choose, including 'Iceberg', 'Dream White', and 'Crystalline'.

'Lady Banks' Rose (Rosa Banksiae)—In the right setting, this old garden rose is lovely with massed clusters of tiny white flowers in great profusion in spring (there's also a yellow version). However, unless you own an estate or a very, very long fence, you'll be sorry you included it because it grows to massive proportions in a relatively short time. There's one plant in Tombstone, Arizona, that made it into the *Guinness Book of World Records* as the world's largest rose plant, sprawling more than eight thousand square feet.

'Tropicana'—Clear coral color and sweet fragrance continue to attract rose lovers worldwide to this venerable hybrid tea rose. However, if you live west of the Rocky Mountains, beware. This rose will succumb to mildew and rust. Instead, use the vigorous shrub 'Oranges 'N' Lemons' or hybrid teas 'Bing Crosby', 'Cary Grant', or 'Lucille Ball'.

'Sterling Silver'—This is a beloved lavender hybrid tea that has graced gardens for decades. However, the plant is so prone to mildew that it isn't worthy of a garden spot now because better lavender varieties like 'Barbra Streisand' or 'Stainless Steel' are available.

Roses for Cold Climates

ROSE GROWERS IN CLIMATE ZONES 3 AND 4 (see USDA chart on page 151) have a tough time growing most modern hybrid tea and floribunda roses. Severe freezing winters mean a lot of work to overwinter and protect these plants. Fortunately for them, research in Canada has resulted in repeat blooming roses with inherent hardiness. Called Explorer and Morden series, they will live and flourish under these harsh conditions, as will the Buck series, developed in the U.S.

Here are some recommended varieties:

'Carefree Beauty'—Developed by Dr. Griffith Bucks at Iowa State University, the profusely blooming shrub is winter-hardy in Iowa without protection. Fragrant rose-pink flowers are large and profuse. Orange hips appear in fall. The plant is very resistant to blackspot and mildew.

'Champlain'—Profuse clusters of dark velvety red flowers characterize this very disease-resistant plant. Bright orange hips in fall extend the colorful display.

'Golden Wings'—This large shrub has single yellow flowers that bloom early in spring and continue almost nonstop to fall. It is fragrant and has great disease resistance, too.

'John Cabot'—This climbing rose has good disease resistance and blossoms in deep orchid pink.

'John Davis'—A small climber or large shrub, it has pink flowers in profusion on a plant with very good disease resistance.

'Lambert Closse'—Copious quantities of pale pink double flowers appear on this moderately sized plant with dark green, disease-resistant glossy leaves.

'Mrs. Doreen Pike'—Developed by David Austin, this English rose is a rugosa, which means it has inherent disease resistance and outstanding hardiness. Pink fragrant flowers are large, with a ruffled, rosette form.

'George Vancouver'—This small, vigorous variety produces quantities of red, semi-double flowers that cover the plant. It sets hips in fall for added visual color.

'Prairie Joy'—Its lovely pink double blooms repeat during the growing season. The plant is dense and spreads to about four feet. It has excellent hardiness and disease resistance.

'Morden Sunrise'—The single orange-yellow flowers have wavy petals and yellow stamens. As they age, the colors change from dark orange to light orange to creamy yellow. Excellent disease resistance and hardiness make this an excellent choice for cold climates.

Roses for Hot Climates

ROSE GROWING IS SIMPLIFIED when you grow roses that are suited to your particular climate. For example, roses with lots of petals need heat to open well. If temperatures aren't high enough, the petals stay closed in the bud stage, a condition termed "balling."

In hot, dry regions, like Southern California, this frequently takes place in spring. Although daytime temperatures can reach eighty degrees or higher, at night there is a significant drop. Very full roses like 'Toro' won't unfurl to display their rich, deep red brilliance. But in the humid South, where nights remain warm, this is a great rose.

Here are ten excellent roses for hot, dry regions:

Hybrid Teas

'Artistry'—Large flowers of soft coral with a hint of cream on the undersides make this medium-tall, upright growing variety one of the most popular around. Leaves are naturally disease-resistant. However, there's little fragrance.

'Brigadoon'—This AARS winner produces fascinating flowers of cream blushing to strawberry coral. A little heat encourages the blushing effect. The plant is vigorous, slightly spreading, with excellent disease resistance. A mild tea fragrance is a bonus.

'Crystalline'—Elegant flowers in clear white show off in any garden. Glossy, dark green, disease-resistant leaves showcase the flowers to great advantage. This is one of the few varieties first developed for the cut flower trade to succeed in garden settings. Expect long stems, and lots of them. There is a medium sweet tea fragrance to enjoy, too.

'Fragrant Cloud'—This is a variety that deserves a place in the garden simply because of its perfume—strong, sweet spice and rose. Vivid coral red-orange flowers are shapely and produced in abundance as the plant matures.

'Ingrid Bergman'—Many rose experts regard this as the best red rose around. Clear red flowers have a lovely form. The plant has glossy dark green foliage, is compact and bushy, and withstands fungal diseases very well. Alas, this glamorous lady doesn't wear perfume—she's lovely to behold but not to sniff.

'Mellow Yellow'—This is one of the best yellow roses on the market because the vivid yellow color won't fade, even on the hottest days. As the plant matures, it produces an abundance of flowers, excellently showcased by deep green leaves that are disease-free.

Floribundas

'Betty Boop'—This nicely rounded AARS-winning plant is one of the easiest roses to grow because it produces loads of colorful, long-lasting flower clusters and is virtually disease-free. The unusual colors start as yellow, edged with vivid red, then fade to whitish ivory and the edging matures to a softer red. The plant sheds its flowers on its own, so there's no need to deadhead. It's quick to send out new canes and flower clusters so there is rarely a time when it's not in bloom. It has a moderately fruity, but not strong, fragrance.

'Hot Cocoa'—This arresting color is sometimes brick, sometimes cocoa, and sometimes a sort of smoky chocolate-orange. No two of these fascinating flowers are alike. The plant is tall and upright, vigorous, and very free-flowering. There's little problem with diseases, and coupled with moderate old rose fragrance, this is an outstanding AARS-winning variety.

'Sheila's Perfume'—What a honey of a rose! The fragrance is enchanting, and the flowers are a fascinating yellow edged with deep pink that blushes as the flower matures. Each nicely shaped flower looks more like a hybrid tea in form. Glossy green leaves have great disease resistance in dry regions. In humidity, however, blackspot is a problem.

Climbers

'Cl. Sally Holmes'—In colder regions, this is a true floribunda. In hot areas, give this showstopper lots of room because it sends out canes ten feet or more in many directions. A true disease-free variety, the plant is useful if you want to cover a large fence or wall. When Sally blooms, she produces immense clusters of ivory to white single flowers. The overall effect is of a hydrangea. And the flower clusters last and last and last on the plant, or if you cut them for indoor enjoyment, they can remain fresh for at least two to three weeks. There isn't much fragrance, but that's easy to forgive since the flower show is so spectacular.

Here are ten roses for hot, humid climates:

'Artistry', 'Brigadoon', 'Crystalline', and **'Ingrid Bergman'** will also thrive in hot, humid regions.

'Bonica'—A proven performer in the landscape, it is the first shrub to win the AARS award because it is vigorous, hardy, produces lots of flowers in clusters, and has exceptional disease resistance.

'Double Delight'—This fragrant hybrid tea combines eye-catching, creamy-white-edged-with-red flowers and fantastic spicy rose fragrance. The red blush intensifies in heat.

'Knock Out'—This lovely shrub is especially prized in humid climates because of its exceptional resistance to blackspot.

'Moonstone'—Huge white flowers edged with light pink on elegant long stems make this classic hybrid tea a standout. This hybrid tea flourishes in climates with hot days and nights when the large blossoms open with stunning form.

'St. Patrick'—The novel greenish tinge to the yellow flowers makes this a standout hybrid tea rose in the garden. Its color holds well in heat, and because the flowers are slow to open, they last, too.

'Toro'—Also known as 'Uncle Joe', this is a remarkable red hybrid tea with numerous (approximately fifty) deep, dark red petals. It needs warm nights as well as hot days for the full blossoms to unfurl.

Branded Roses

IT USED TO BE THAT WHEN YOU WANTED to buy a rose, you chose first by classification—hybrid tea, floribunda, grandiflora, and the like—then by variety. Now, what I like to think of as "branded roses" are changing the whole selection process. Various rose breeders are concentrating on developing series of roses, by linking common characteristics and crossing the demarcations of formal classification.

Several decades ago, David Austin made quite an impact on hybridization by creating what he called English Roses. They combine the flower shape and form of Old Garden Roses with the repeat-flowering of modern roses. There are now more than 120 varieties available in the United States. When they crossed the shores from England, many Austin rose varieties grew larger than expected in warm regions. So many outgrew their space in modern gardens that a search for these new-old roses' more compact bushes intrigued rose hybridizers.

The results are the Romantica series from the venerable French firm Meilland, the Generosa series from Roseraie Guillot, and Shrublets from Weeks Roses. Other notable branded roses are 'Simplicity' from Jackson & Perkins, and Dream roses and Flower Carpet from Anthony Tesselaar.

I've tried some of these branded roses with varied results. Here's a brief description some of my favorites:

Flower Carpet

First introduced in 1995, this series of groundcover roses is available in pink, apple blossom (pastel pink), red, white, coral, and yellow. Characterized by disease resistance and hardiness, these slightly mounding roses rebloom freely in clusters. They live up to their name, providing a carpet of color, either in the ground or in containers. They improve with age, and older plants of five years or more can produce more flowers than you care to count. More than ten million have been sold in the U.S., and they're very popular in Europe where they have won more than fourteen awards. They are widely available at nurseries or by mail order.

Dream Roses

Introduced in 2000, Dream Roses are characterized as floribunda or hybrid tea blooms on compact plants. Bred in the U.S. by Jerry Twomey, they are noted for free flowering, little pruning, and strong disease resistance. I find that they are indeed little flower machines and so far, are performing according to expectations. I'm particularly impressed with 'Dream Orange' and 'Dream Yellow' for their floriferousness. You can also find 'Dream Red' and 'Dream White' with more to come onto the market.

English Roses

These really deliver what they promise—old-fashioned flowers on plants that repeat their blooms and produce very fragrant roses. However, be advised that quite a few are susceptible to diseases, including rust, mildew, or blackspot. Also, in hot climates, you might get more than you planned—some varieties soar in endless sunshine. In my garden, 'Brother Cadfael' exceeded twelve feet with equal spread before I reluctantly removed it to preserve cherished garden space.

Romantica

Introduced by the creator of 'Peace', the Romantica series is marketed as highly fragrant, old-fashioned looking roses on compact shrubs. My experience is that few are as fragrant as touted, at least in my garden. They are indeed compact growers and have good disease resistance and flower form.

Generosa

Under development for a decade, the Generosa roses are an attempt by Guillot to combine their venerable and fragrant Old Garden Roses with modern compact plant sizes. Introduced in 2000, they are, according to reports, fragrant, tough plants, although some of the varieties do need garden space. New varieties will be introduced in succeeding years.

'Simplicity'

Introduced by Jackson & Perkins more than twenty years ago, the 'Simplicity' series became the top sellers in America with more than twenty-one million in the marketplace by now. They were the first of the landscaping roses, and were marketed as "living fences." This hedge concept helped Americans think of roses as useful landscape plants in their own right instead of single specimens. Pink was the first available, and now you can also select white, red, purple, or yellow. They're characterized by very good disease resistance and rapid repeat bloom. They need only shaping and light pruning.

Towne & Country

From Poulsen Roses, this series includes twenty-six varieties ranging from groundcovers to four-foot shrubs. All share the characteristics of masses of small flowers that are self-cleaning. Poulsen developed these shrub roses for use in mass landscapes or grouping in containers. They are very disease-resistant and free-flowering varieties that need pruning just to shape once every year or two, depending on location.

Shrublets

The distinction between miniature roses and full-size roses keeps getting harder and harder to determine as bush sizes continue to grow. Basically, the term miniature refers to the flower size on the shrub. Weeks Roses is attempting to aid the consumer understand the size and scale by classifying several of its varieties as 'Shrublets'. 'Gourmet Popcorn', 'Raven', 'Rocking Robin', 'What A Peach', and 'Baby Love' are readily available and will be joined by more in time. These versatile plants add easy color to gardens or containers and are a wonderful way to add a lot of flowers to the scene without much fuss.

Did you know that roses can get freckles? Like some people who spot in sunlight, light, colored roses get spots of color, but they're reddish instead of brown. White, light pink, and lavender roses get spots of color in certain weather conditions such as cool nights followed by hot days. The solution is to cut the buds when they're one-third open and enjoy them indoors.

Red, White, and Blue Roses

ON SEPTEMBER 11, 2001, when the sorrow and heartbreak became unbearable, I found solace in my rose garden. Like many people who know the value of garden therapy, I tore out weeds, removed fading flowers, dug up some companion plants that were past their prime, and literally stopped to smell the roses.

It helped. The images didn't fade from my mind, but the very act of tearing out invasive weeds and overgrown plants helped me feel like there's at least a small part of life that's under control. Planting something beautiful cheers the spirit. Tending a garden means there's one small part of the world in which an individual can make a difference.

One type of garden statement evokes a patriotic atmosphere with the red, white, and blue colors of the nation's flag in bloom. Although a true blue rose doesn't exist yet, you can suggest the color with one or two pretenders. (You might want to include other kinds of blue flowers as well, such as salvia). If you have a lot of space, consider making a design statement in a garden bed or as a border. Or you might plant a rose bush in a large container on a deck, patio, or balcony. Here are some varieties appropriate for this purpose because of their colors or names.

Red

'Crimson Glory'—This hybrid tea has proven its worth in the garden since it was introduced in 1935. Its dark velvet crimson flowers emit a rich damask fragrance. This variety thrives in warm climates where it can grow very tall.

'Proud Land'—Growing in gardens since 1969, this tried-and-true hybrid tea is a bushy plant that produces long-stemmed flowers with a slight scent.

'Veterans' Honor'—Brilliant red, classic hybrid tea flowers are produced on elegant long stems. This variety has strong disease resistance and a striking raspberry fragrance. Jackson & Perkins introduced this variety in 2000 and donates 10 percent of sales to a veterans' health care fund.

White

'Honor'—The crystal white flowers of this long-stemmed, elegant hybrid tea have classic high-centered form, giving it a fitting name. Fragrance is light; disease resistance is very good.

Blue

'Outta the Blue'—Introduced in 2002, this new shrub may not exactly be a blue rose, but it's the one closest to blue right now. The blue hues range from lavender-blue to multi-toned magenta on this free-flowering shrub with a strong clove and rose scent. It has very good disease resistance.

'Purple Heart'—This purple-red floribunda has strong fragrance and produces Old Garden Rose form flowers.

Red and White

'Cl. Fourth of July'—An award-winning climber, this rose bears abundant numbers of velvety red and bright white striped roses. No two flowers are alike. Give this bush room, for in time it will produce canes ten to fourteen feet long.

Other Colors

Although their color theme isn't exactly red, white, or blue, the names of these roses make them likely candidates for a patriotic garden:

'Peace'—One of the most beloved roses of the twentieth century, this rose symbolized the hope for lasting peace after World War II. Its colors are lemon yellow edged with pure pink. 'Peace' is easy to grow and still very much worthy of space in a garden.

'Cl. America'—Coral pink roses bloom in abundance on this climber and emit a wonderful, spicy fragrance. This popular rose is susceptible to mildew when weather is overcast, but its other virtues outweigh the disease factor.

Grow a Bouquet of Roses

ONE OF THE JOYS OF GROWING ROSES is gathering them to make lovely bouquets. I always admire people with time and talent who craft dramatic, lush bouquets that spill out of their containers.

Alas, I spend more time in the garden or writing about gardening than I devote to flower arranging. However, I've discovered that some rose varieties become instant bouquets when I cut a few stems and place them in a lovely crystal vase.

The rose varieties that do this best are the ones that produce flowers in large clusters or sprays. Stem length should also be long enough for vase display. This eliminates many climbing roses with lovely flowers but short stems. So, too, floribunda roses, which by definition bear flowers in clusters, tend to produce them on short stems.

Instant floral arrangers can have their bouquets with lots of time to spare by careful selection of cooperative varieties. My hands-down favorite is a relatively new rose called 'Cl. Berries 'n' Cream'. A spectacular rose that flowers on new and old wood, this climber is rarely out of bloom. In my garden, it produces masses of deep pink and white striped flowers on long stems. The plant produces flower clusters with four to eight flowers in each. Just a few stems really create an instant bouquet. Flowers last a long time, too—at least ten days. The only downside is that there's a very subtle fragrance. To enhance nose allure, I tuck in one or two very strongly scented roses, such as the hybrid tea 'Secret' or the grandiflora 'Lagerfeld'.

Another of my favorite bouquet roses is 'Sally Holmes', another massive climbing vari-

ety, at least in warm regions where one plant can grow twenty feet. It produces large clusters of single, white flowers that resemble hydrangeas. Flowers last a long time, even up to two weeks. In colder regions of the country, this rose grows only to four or five feet, behaving like the floribunda that it is classified as. Another climbing rose that works in a similar way is an AARS winner, 'Cl. Fourth of July'. This striking rose has clusters of single flowers striped with brilliant red, yellow, and white.

You can also look to floribundas for bouquet roses. Try 'Blueberry Hill', a soft lavender rose with pretty yellow stamens. For a vivid presentation, 'Playboy' offers a deep orange and red blend. Or, you can select one of its offspring, 'Playgirl', which has double flowers in a deep pink. An AARS winner in 1999, 'Betty Boop' is an eye-catching yellow floribunda with red-edged double flowers. It blooms so freely that it will easily provide you with stems for an arrangement and lots more on the plant for garden display. If you prefer a softer pink, try older floribunda varieties such as 'Sexy Rexy' or 'Gene Boerner'.

Good red roses are hard to find, especially when you want to fill a vase with them. Hybrid tea roses tend to produce eight, ten, or twelve blooms in each cycle, scarcely enough to harvest for a lavish bouquet. However, there's 'Crimson Bouquet', a vigorous grandiflora that produces scarlet red blossoms in enough profusion for arrangements and garden display.

For white, it's hard to beat 'Iceberg', a floribunda that blooms and blooms and blooms.

A little patience is needed for all these varieties. It takes a few years for bushes to establish themselves before they bloom in great numbers. I think it's worth the wait.

Preserve Your Bouquet

To preserve the vase life of cut roses, add a few drops of liquid bleach and a teaspoon of sugar to the vase water. Cut off any leaves that will be underwater to reduce bacterial formation.

Heritage Roses for Modern Gardens

MANY GARDENERS ADMIRE the intense fragrance, romantic history, and informal growth habits of heritage roses, also dubbed antique roses and officially classified as Old Garden Roses (OGRs). Their major distinction is that rather than having the upright, high-centered shape of modern hybrid tea roses, these flowers are usually cupped, ruffled, or quartered. In general, they also grow larger than modern roses.

Detractors of heritage roses point out that many types are very large, can require staking or pegging, and can overwhelm today's small urban gardens. A large number are also prone to diseases like mildew, rust, or blackspot. Heritage roses commonly have blossoms that can open and shatter within several days. This fleeting beauty doesn't matter to those who enjoy them on bushes rather than for indoor display. Although individual flowers come and go quickly, bushes can produce so many that the landscape remains lovely. Some types, too, bloom just once during the year, unlike modern roses developed for longer bloom periods. Fans of heritage roses respond that they are tough plants, as evidenced by the vigorous ones still flourishing in abandoned homesteads or cemeteries. They also claim that heritage roses sold today are the best of the best because they have stood the test of time. The following describes the classifications of OGRs.

Albas—These white or blush pink, very fragrant flowers on tall, upright bushes with gray-green foliage are spring flowering. Very hardy and disease-resistant, they thrive in cold climates.

Bourbons—Popular in Victorian England, the large, fragrant blooms grow on vigorous bushes. Many varieties have repeat flowering.

Centifolias—Also called cabbage roses, these were especially popular in Holland where their multi-petaled beauty was depicted in paintings. In spring, heavily fragrant flowers bloom in pink or cerise. These are large, arching plants.

Chinas—These were introduced to Europe in the mid-eighteenth century. Small to low-growing shrubs produce clusters of small flowers ranging from white, to pink, to true scarlet. Their fragrance is spicier than other OGRs and they're noted for repeat blooming and being cold tender. They're excellent for warm regions.

Damasks—Brought to Europe by the crusaders, these ancient roses have rich perfume. The tall, arching shrubs do well in colder regions.

Gallicas—Among the oldest roses, these short, compact plants have thin, prickly canes. They can spread vigorously. Heavily perfumed flowers range in color from pale pink to dark purple. Some are striped. They're spring flowering and winter-hardy.

Hybrid perpetuals—Popular in Victorian England, these repeat blooms of fragrant, full flowers grow on tall, upright shrubs.

Moss roses—Also popular in Victorian England, these distinctive roses have fragrant, mosslike growth on the flower buds that display a range of colors and flower forms. Moss roses do better in colder regions.

Noisettes—Hybridized more than 150 years ago in South Carolina, these repeat-blooming, fragrant plants are often used as climbing or pillar roses. They're excellent in hot climates.

Portlands—More compact than damasks, the very fragrant, repeat-blooming Portlands do exceptionally well in small gardens.

Ramblers and climbers—Some are so vigorous that they grow into treetops. Although most are once-blooming, they produce masses of show-stopping blooms. Some are fragrant.

Rugosa—These are excellent for coastal gardens because they withstand salt-laden air. Very cold-hardy, fragrant, and disease-resistant. Species bloom once, hybrids repeat. Many produce hips in winter.

Species roses—These are the original roses that grow wild in temperate climates and have characteristic flowers of five petals.

Teas—Developed in China, and named because the scent of these roses resembles fresh crushed tea leaves, this group's flowers are larger than their China relatives. The large, open plants have fragile stems and are best for warm climates.

Within these classifications, many varieties are available. Those who live and garden in the warm South or West will have better success with tea, China, Portland, and noisette varieties because they are restrained in size and prefer warm climates.

Like their modern relatives, heritage rose bushes need sun, water, a little fertilizer, and some shaping or training. Plant in a sunny location that receives at least six hours of sunlight. Roses in hot regions can benefit from protection from afternoon sun. 'Old Blush' will grow in part shade. Although they can flourish in poor soil, they're at their best in fertile, well-draining soil liberally amended with rotted manure, aged compost, or similar organic matter.

Heritage roses can grow without much water, but will thrive with a deep soaking every week or ten days, depending on temperatures. Mulch is an essential garden component to conserve water, cool roots, and control weeds. Add two to four inches of compost, leaf mulch, or any other organic material. Fertilize regularly, but not too heavily. By selecting varieties that are naturally disease-resistant, it's not necessary to spray to combat rose diseases.

In general, most antique roses bloom just once a year, on wood produced the previous year. So, they need to be pruned differently than modern roses. The best time to prune is six weeks after they've finished flowering. Remove dead canes, and depending on variety, prune to shape the plant. Varieties that produce long canes can be pegged. Gently bend the cane to the ground, and tie it to a stake or an adjoining cane. This encourages flower formation along the cane length for increased flower production.

Best OGRs for cold climates

'Alba', semi-plena (White Rose of York) (Alba, ancient), white, 7' x 5'

'Apothecary's Rose', gallica, red-purple, 4' x 4'

'Belle Isis', gallica, pale pink, 4' x 3'

'Leda', damask, white, edged red, 3' x 3'

'Madame Hardy', damask, white, 5' x 5'

'Petite de Holland', centifolia, pink, 4' x 3'

'Rosa Mundi', gallica, pink striped, 3' x 3'

'Rugosa Rubra', rugosa, red, 7' x 6'

'Tuscany' (Velvet Rose), gallica, wine red, 3' x 3'

'York and Lancaster', damask, cream and pink, 5' x 4'

Best OGRs for warm climates

'Baronne Prevost', hybrid perpetual, pink, 6' x 6'

'Cl Cecile Brunner', climbing, polyantha pink, to 25'

'Duchesse de Brabant', tea, pink, 4' x 6'

'Dutchess of Portland', crimson, 3' x 3'

'Green Rose', China, green, 4' x 4'

'Lady Hillingdon', tea, yellow, 6' x 4'

'Mutabilis', China, yellow/red/apricot, 6' x 6'

'Old Blush', China, pink, 3' x 4'

'Reine de Violette', hybrid perpetual, purple-pink, 6' x 6'

'Souvenir de la Malmaison', bourbon, shell pink, 3' x 3'

Experts have identified at least twenty-five different rose fragrances, including cinnamon, apple, clove, and musk. Roses can smell bad, too, if their ancestry includes the yellow species rose R. foetida.

Why Are Roses Fragrant?

WHAT'S THE FIRST REACTION MOST PEOPLE have to the sight of a rose? If you're like me, you lean into the blossom, inhale deeply, and expect to be rewarded with a heavenly scent. And what a delight when this gesture is rewarded with alluring damask, tantalizing spice, sweet citrus, anise, or other scents that roses can offer. But how disappointing when there isn't any fragrance at all.

Like many flowers, roses are fragrant, or are supposed to be fragrant, not to delight human noses but to attract pollinators so that the plant can reproduce. Contrary to popular belief, roses are just as fragrant now as they've ever been. It's just that detecting fragrances depends on the rose variety, its location, and weather.

I spoke with several famous rose breeders to get their insights into just what goes into making a rose fragrant. "Fragrance is extremely complicated with lots of genes involved," explained Keith Zary, the hybridizer for Jackson & Perkins roses. "Volatile compounds— some oils and some alcohols—all contribute to rose fragrance. They're usually located in glands at the base of the petals, and their release into the air makes it possible for us to enjoy the aroma."

The best time to detect these enticing scents is on a calm day, when the rose plant has been well watered, but the blossom itself is dry and the temperature isn't too hot. Usually, at ten in the morning and again in late afternoon the volatile oils are easiest to detect. Even a rose with powerful fragrance may seem lacking in scent on a hot, dry day when winds are blowing. The Santa Ana wind conditions in Southern California can often make roses not as nose-worthy. One way around this situation is to cut the blooms and bring them indoors where they'll release their aroma.

Because the scent glands are located in petals, varieties with thick, waxy petals can be almost completely lacking in fragrance. That's one reason why very fragrant varieties have been quick to deteriorate as the fragile petals decay quickly. According to Tom Carruth, in the recent past, fragrance had been linked with disease problems. "We've been able to create fragrant varieties that are a lot cleaner than older fragrant roses," he said. An example is 'Sterling Silver', a beloved lavender rose with powerful Old Rose fragrance. But it's also very prone to mildew. Fortunately, breeders have created new disease-resistant lavender, mauve, and purple varieties, including 'Barbra Streisand', 'Purple Heart', 'Moon Shadow', and 'Melody Parfumee'. All are extremely fragrant and have tough foliage that withstands the onslaughts of mildew and rust.

Fragrance can be linked to flower color. In general, yellow roses can produce citrus or anise aromas. Red and deep pinks can emit the heavy damask scent associated with Old Garden Roses. Lavenders can produce citrus scents. This is only a generalization because roses can have complicated genetic backgrounds, such as the white rose 'White Lightnin' ', which produces a strong citrus aroma because it has yellow in its background.

If you'd like to include some powerfully aromatic roses in your garden, consider the following, suggested by Zary and Carruth:

'Barbra Streisand'—purple hybrid tea

'Cotillion'—lavender English style shrub

'Fragrant Lace'—light pink hybrid tea with yellow reverse on petals

'French Perfume'—yellow and pink blend hybrid tea

'Full Sail'—white hybrid tea

'Melody Parfumee'—lavender hybrid tea

'Moon Shadow'—dusky lavender hybrid tea

'Purple Heart'—wine-red floribunda

'Rose Rhapsody'—dusky lavender hybrid tea

'Scentimental'—red and white striped floribunda

'Sheila's Perfume'—yellow-edged with deep pink floribunda

'Shocking Blue'—medium lavender floribunda

'Veterans' Honor'—red hybrid tea

'White Lightnin' '—white grandiflora

Romantica Roses
old-fashioned flowers on modern bushes

T HE ALLURE OF OLD-FASHIONED FLOWER FORMS and intoxicating
fragrances are tempting many rose lovers to grow David Austin English
Roses, which have been emigrating to America from their native England for almost two
decades. More than 120 varieties of these modern versions of antique roses exist. I've found
that in sunny Southern California, many varieties explode in height and width and have to
be grown as climbing roses. Some, like 'Graham Thomas', can soar to fifteen feet, causing
many a frustrated rose lover to banish them from their gardens and replace them with varieties that won't swallow so much garden space.

Now, from France, comes a new rose series that also promises old-fashioned allure and
fragrance, but on smaller bushes with more disease resistance. They are named the Romantica series, and have been created by the House of Meilland, the venerable rose firm best
known for the 'Peace' rose, and distributed in America by Canard-Pyle Star Roses Company.

In development for more than fifteen years, Romantica roses are starting to make their
way into high-end nurseries and are also available on the Internet at www.starroses.com.
The House of Meilland, located in the sun-drenched hills of Provence, sought to create
roses that would thrive in the rigorous sunshine of the region and also offer strong fragrances. The breeders consulted with nearby fragrance companies to understand the
alchemy of essences.

The result is more than a dozen already on the market, with promises of more in years to come. These are some of the most noteworthy:

'Abbaye de Cluny', named for a famous Catholic monastery in France, grows to about five feet. The apricot, ruffled, and cupped flowers have a strong, spicy scent.

'August Renoir' grows to the same height. Deep pink, very fragrant flowers are cupped and quartered.

'Frederick Mistral', named for a Nobel-winning poet and writer, resembles a hybrid tea in form, but opens to a cup shape. It combines sweet fragrance and good disease resistance with strong reblooming characteristics. It is the most vigorous of the Romantica series and can grow to six feet or more.

'Guy de Maupassant', named for the French dramatist, is a soft pink floribunda with globe-shaped buds. They open to three-inch full and double blossoms. The fragrance is apple, which may be too subtle to be detected by some noses. The bushy plant reblooms well throughout the year.

'Toulouse-Lautrec', named for the famous artist, produces clear yellow flowers with a lemon verbena fragrance. It, too, has good disease resistance.

'Francois Rabelias' is a floribunda with clusters of scarlet red quartered blooms. The plant is compact.

'Jean Giorno' is a vigorous grandiflora with blossoms that open in the shape of a large dahlia. Each petal is veined in red, and the flowers emit strong spice and clove fragrances.

'Tchiakovsky' has large old-fashioned blooms that are creamy white with buttery yellow centers. It also offers strong disease resistance.

Romantica roses can be grown as any hybrid tea or shrub. Plant in full sun, fertilize, water regularly, and prune to shape. Although you may be tempted to gather the first flush of blooms to enjoy in a bouquet, be patient and leave them on the plant for the first flowering cycle so that the plant can grow stronger.

Roses That Trap Dogs
and small children

HAVE YOU BEEN IN A CAR ACCIDENT?" a friend exclaimed when viewing my newly scarred arms.

"No, I've just been pruning a climbing rose with especially wicked thorns," I replied.

Not long after that event, I decided that getting impaled by fierce rose thorns wasn't part of the fun of growing roses. I'd always been able to tolerate rose thorns—after all, I like to think the plant is just being friendly and grabbing a passerby for attention. But some roses have thorns like fish hooks, as did the offending climber 'Dortmund' that grew rampantly along my fence. Although renowned for beautiful red blooms with lovely white centers and long, graceful canes, 'Dortmund' is also notorious for its dangerously long thorns. I removed it from my garden and decided never to grow roses that could be classified as deadly weapons.

Thorns, or prickles, occur on almost every rose variety—antique or modern. Early Christian legends say that roses didn't have thorns until Adam sinned in the Garden of Eden. A less poetic explanation is that roses probably evolved this defense mechanism to prevent being eaten by animals. Another theory is that thorns trap moisture close to the stem. Whatever the reason, people who enjoy growing roses certainly don't want their flesh trapped close to the stem, and some people even avoid growing roses altogether for this very reason.

A few precautions make growing roses worthwhile, even with their thorns. Keep in mind the Arab proverb "Don't be angry because the thorn bush has thorns. Be happy it has roses." One commonsense approach is to wear garden gloves when working around rose bushes. When winter pruning season arrives, be sure to wear a long-sleeved shirt or sweat-shirt (preferably an old one because it's certain that little holes will appear). That was the mistake I had made—I wandered amidst the canes of 'Dortmund' wearing a short-sleeved shirt enjoying the lovely, balmy December day.

You can also select varieties with few or no thorns. In response to gardeners' desires for "ouchless" roses, some hybridizers have bred for this specific trait. Monrovia Nursery, one of the largest wholesale growers in America, offers a series of roses called 'Smooth'. Developed by Harvey Davidson of Western Sun Roses, these are ninety-eight percent thorn-free. The series has several varieties in colors including white, cream, pink, and red. A few are fragrant. Check with your local nursery for availability.

Sometimes thorny roses can be a real plus. Grow some climbers, like 'Dortmund' or 'Altissimo', on fences or around windows as barriers to burglars. The small shrub rose 'Sir Thomas Lipton' has stiff prickly stems that form an impenetrable barrier, which makes an excellent hedge when you want to deter intruders or animals. Some of the David Austin English roses can also serve a similar function. A few groundcover roses are also very thorny and can be useful barriers.

For your general gardening pleasure, consider the stems before you choose a rose based only on its blooms. Thorniness can be an important factor in selection if you have young children or pets and want to safeguard them. The downside of ordering from catalogues or the Internet is that you can see only the flower. See the actual bushes in bloom at public gardens, nurseries, and garden centers to be sure that the entire plant is suited to your garden.

Here are some additional thornless roses to consider for your garden:

'Lady Banks'—a species—*Rosa banksia* is white, *Rosa banksia lutea* is yellow. This is a very large climbing rose that produces masses of clustered small flowers in profusion during spring. Completely thornless.

'J.P. Connell'—white shrub rose that grows very well in cold climates.

'Mme. Legras de St. Germain'—This antique Alba has large creamy white flowers on a plant growing seven feet tall.

'Reine des Violettes'—a Hybrid Perpetual that has many clusters of very fragrant reddish-purple flowers. Plant is rounded and grows to about four feet. Its flowers last just a few days, but the plant reblooms well.

'Zephirine Drouhin'—climbing Bourbon rose that grows seven feet high and wide. Deep rose pink flowers are very fragrant and are produced in great quantities. Plant may be prone to disease in cool climates.

'Sally Holmes'—A floribunda that grows as a large climber in frost-free areas, this thornless plant produces large clusters of creamy white flowers that last a long time on the plant or in a vase.

'Knock Out'—a delightful shrub that's well behaved in any garden setting. Completely free of disease, including blackspot, this hardy shrub has lots of bright red or deep pink single roses in clusters.

Old Friends in the Rose Garden

WHEN I WAS A YOUNGSTER AT CAMP, one of my favorite camp-fire songs was the round "Make new friends and keep the old—one is silver and the other gold."

I recalled this piece of nostalgia when I looked at my rose garden one day. In my need to view the latest rose varieties, I had parted with some of my favorite friends in the rose kingdom. Roses that had been my pride and joy twenty years ago are no longer in my landscape. So, I decided to bring back a few of my old friends to share places of glory with their new relatives.

New is novel, maybe new is better, but there certainly are modern roses that are still worthy of places in our gardens. My criteria for roses are that they bloom in abundance, are eye-catching, offer some scent, and are disease-resistant. It's true that rose breeders keep bringing us new and improved versions of past glories. But it's also true that there are some really great roses that wear well with age. One is 'Peace', the rose that symbolized the end of World War II. Since its introduction in 1946, 'Peace' has continued to attract fans who appreciate the large lemon yellow blooms edged with pure pink. This is such an easy bush to grow that it remains a wonderful garden choice.

In the 1950s, several notable roses catapulted to fame and are still great roses. The white floribunda 'Iceberg' still rates among the world's top ten roses. 'Chrysler Imperial' continues to be one of the best fragrant red hybrid teas. Happily for me, this variety thrives in hot climates.

Yellow roses usually languish in hot climates. Yet 'King's Ransom', introduced in 1962, can still hold her own among the newer yellow varieties. Another top performer is 'Duet', introduced in 1961. This two-toned pink hybrid tea is a real workhorse in the garden, producing loads of large, ruffled blossoms. Easy to grow and vigorous, this is one of the best varieties for people who don't want to fuss over their roses. 'Mister Lincoln' is another beloved variety from the 1960s. With velvety deep red flowers and strong damask rose fragrance, this hybrid tea continues to be one of the most popular reds. Another great rose, also from the 1960s, is the sweetly fragrant grandiflora 'White Lightnin''. I once counted close to 150 crystal white flowers on this super plant. An added bonus is its sweet citrus scent.

If fragrance is your most important request from a modern rose, consider the hybrid tea 'Perfume Delight', which has been wooing noses since her introduction in 1974. Hot pink flowers emit strong damask rose fragrance on a vigorous plant. Another '70s charmer is 'Playboy', a floribunda with bright single blossoms of orange and scarlet with a yellow center. Although the fragrance is slight, the flower show is spectacular. I'm a fan of the "hand-painted" series of roses created by hybridizer Sam McGredy. One of my favorites is 'Regensberg', a floribunda from 1979. The compact plant covers itself with masses of bright white flowers splashed with hot pink. It's perfect for small borders or containers. Another colorful dazzler from the '70s is 'Double Delight', a two-toned hybrid tea of cream blushing yellow edged with red. With strong fragrance and striking flowers, it still merits a place in twenty-first-century landscapes.

One of my all-time favorites is 'Lagerfeld', which I've grown since it was introduced in 1986. This stately grandiflora rose produces bouquets of elegant, long-stemmed silvery lilac roses with a heavenly citrus aroma. Quick to repeat its bloom cycle, the bush will grow quite tall in warm climates.

Left: 'Iceberg' is regarded as one of the top ten roses in the world. This floribunda is excellent in mass plantings or as a focal point by itself.

Below: 'Scentimental' has it all—great fragrance, loads of unusually colored blossoms, and superb disease resistance.

Opposite: 'White Simplicity' is a floribunda marketed as a living fence. Along with its red, pink, or yellow relatives in the Simplicity line, this is an easy-care plant great for mass displays.

Opposite: 'Cl. America' is a proven performer that won an AARS award in 1976. A little later to flower than other varieties, it offers coral pink flowers with tantalizing spicy fragrance.

Left: 'Galway Bay' produces trusses of fragrant medium-pink flowers in abundance.

Above: Climbing roses can frame entryways or scenic vistas.

Left: An AARS winner in 1998, 'Fame' is a grandiflora that's a real garden work-horse, producing lots of flowers and dark green leaves.

Below left: This dazzler, 'Tequila Sunrise', is popular in Europe and New Zealand. It won England's Royal National Rose Society Gold Medal in 1988.

Below right: 'Nicole' is a German import. A tall floribunda in cold regions, it reaches skyward in warm climates. It is vigorous and disease-resistant, with masses of jewel-like flowers of white edged red. The color intensifies as flowers age.

Opposite: 'Mikado' is an award-winning hybrid tea rose (AARS 1988) bred in Japan. The rich red blossoms are accented by deep green, glossy leaves.

Opposite: The buds of 'St. Patrick' have distinct green hues in hot weather as they slowly unfurl into lovely golden blooms. It was a 1996 AARS winner.

Above left: At times 'Hot Cocoa' is smoky, at times it's deep rust. Sometimes the color of this AARS 2003 winner is indescribable, but it is a superb rose for any occasion.

Above right: 'Dream Orange' really does live up to its name. Developed by Anthony Tesselaar, this floribunda flowers freely and has excellent disease resistance.

Left: A vibrant floribunda, 'Playboy' has large clusters of scarlet and gold flowers. It is disease-resistant and free-flowering but needs winter protection in cold climates.

Left: 'Pretty Jessica' is a popular David Austin English Rose variety because the plant stays small—about two to three feet—and is great in small gardens or containers.

Below: 'Playgirl' is a proven performer, producing clusters of hot-pink flowers throughout the flowering season. The plant is rounded, of medium height, and has very good disease resistance.

Opposite: 'Paradise' is a heavenly blend of lavender edged with ruby red that deepens with heat. This very fragrant hybrid tea has been a popular choice since it won the AARS award in 1979.

Opposite: 'Opening Night' produces clear red flowers in classic hybrid tea form. Best color and form comes when temperatures are cool. The medium-tall plant has glossy dark green foliage and good disease resistance.

Left: 'Berries 'n' Cream' is a free-flowering climber with light apple fragrance and good disease resistance.

Below: 'Showbiz' is a compact floribunda and an excellent choice for small gardens or containers. The plant produces fire-engine red flowers in profusion.

Opposite: 'Martha's Vineyard' is one of the Poulsen series of Towne and Country Roses, best used in a landscape.

Above left: An import from Germany, 'Lavaglut' means "lava glow." And glow it does, with velvety, dark red flowers.

Above right: 'Graham Thomas' is a tall shrub or very big climber, depending on locale. The deep yellow flowers hold their color, even in summer heat.

Left: 'Cl. Fourth of July', a 1999 AARS-winning climber, produces large red flowers striped with white.

Flower Carpet Roses

IMAGINE A CARPET OF RED, SHELL PINK, or white flowers beautifying your landscape. If this sounds enticing, and you're looking for easy-care roses for landscape or containers, consider Flower Carpet roses. This series of free-flowering, disease-resistant roses has rapidly become the biggest selling rose in America, surpassing the floribunda series marketed as 'Simplicity'. Since their introduction seven years ago, more than ten million Flower Carpet plants have been sold in the U.S., and millions more are blooming in Europe, New Zealand, South Africa, and Australia.

Werner Noack, a German rose breeder who concentrates on creating disease-resistant hybrids, bred the Flower Carpet series. This groundcover rose series consists of pink, white, appleblossom, red, and coral. More colors will be marketed in the future. This rose is easy to find in nurseries and garden centers because it's packaged in a pink pot.

Its virtues include very strong disease resistance, a long flowering period, and the ability to cover itself in massive clusters consisting of small blossoms. Each plant can produce several thousand flowers during the growing season.

I wondered if this was an exaggerated claim, so I spoke with Dan Davids, a local spokesman for Anthony Tesselaar International, distributor for Flower Carpet. He assured me that the claim is true.

"I grow them myself in my own garden and they really do produce thousands of flowers on each plant during the year," Davids said during a phone interview.

The spectacular flower display comes in part from the profuse clusters that each bush can produce, provided they're in sunny locations and given appropriate water and fertilizer. Davids says a common mistake is that people overfertilize with a popular brand of liquid fertilizer applied through a hose-end sprayer.

"This is the worst thing to give Flower Carpet or other roses because it causes vegetative growth and scanty flowers," he explained. "A person can tell if this is the problem when the plant produces long runners with no flowers."

Instead, he suggests applying a three-month time-release, polyon-coated fertilizer in spring, summer, and fall. This approach encourages the plant to bloom profusely in clusters. They also need ample water, especially when grown in containers. Davids says they perform a little better in the ground because the plants produce long roots that can develop better in soil than in pots.

They are very disease-resistant, although occasionally mildew can be a problem. It's not necessary to spray; however, insects can attack these and any other rose, so hosing them off with water or applying a nontoxic insecticide may be necessary.

Pruning these roses is also a cinch because the plants are sterile. That is, they won't set rose hips (seeds) and their flowers fall off when bloom is over. They just need shearing once a year, in December or January, to give them a good start for the next year of growth. Davids uses hedge shears to trim and shape each bush to the size of a basketball.

Flower Carpet roses make strong statements as colorful garden plants. But don't expect exhibition-quality flowers. They've been developed as landscape roses for which high centers or pointed buds aren't the definition of their beauty. In a way, this is one of the exciting things about growing roses. There is an amazing diversity of flower shapes, forms, and sizes available—something to suit a variety of uses.

Tree Roses
add second-story color and fragrance

ONE OF MY FAVORITE PARTS OF THE GARDEN is a flower border at the front of my house containing the fragrant miniature 'Sweet Chariot'. I love this diminutive rose for its old-fashioned form, cascading growth habit, and sweet scent. What particularly delights me is that it grows as a tree rose and when I want to savor its delicious aroma, I only have to lean forward.

I started growing roses with twelve hybrid tea and grandiflora bushes, then rapidly accumulated more than one hundred different rose plants as I increased my collection of hybrid teas, floribundas, grandifloras, climbers, and miniatures tucked into the front of my borders when I ran out of room for the larger varieties. I had bypassed tree roses, technically called "standards," because I hadn't been captivated by what seemed to be unsightly, bare shanks topped with ungainly foliage and flowers. But when I saw miniature roses grown as trees creatively underplanted with mini rose shrubs and companion plants, I was captivated by their charm and practicality.

Like most people, my automatic response to a flower is to bend down and sniff it. This can cause some comical contortions when I want to enjoy the fragrance of a miniature rose growing one or two feet from the ground. Elevating roses to nose and eye level is definitely more convenient. And that's precisely what an increasing number of garden enthusiasts are doing by including tree roses in their landscapes. Originating in Europe in the nineteenth century, tree roses have proliferated in popularity and numbers in recent years in the United States and now account for ten to fifteen percent of all roses sold in the U.S. They consist of two rose bushes budded on top of a length of bare rootstock. They're available in a variety of heights, ranging from miniature roses on twelve-inch or eighteen-inch trunks to floribundas, hybrid teas, or grandifloras budded on two- or three-foot rootstock.

Unfortunately, many people don't use them effectively in their home landscapes. If they're planted in rigid rows along a walkway or driveway, they display naked, unsightly trunks fully visible to the eye. I find that this type of planting doesn't do justice to their potential beauty. They are wonderful along a walkway, but the trick is to underplant them with lower growing roses or companion plants that hide their bare limbs.

Bright mounds of color, tree roses are also an effective way to provide two-story color in a flower border. Some knowledgeable landscapers arrange them at the back of a planting to create a crescendo of height and color. Tree roses can also be tucked into a rose garden where the bushes are closely planted and there's just enough room for roots and the slender trunk. The second story of color above shrub level provides a way to add that "must have" variety where only air space is available. That's what I've been doing in my already crowded garden, and I'm delighted with the results.

Tree roses are more often valuable in a landscape for their splashes of color than for rose clippings since their growth habits often result in flowers on shorter stems. They are excellent choices for large containers displayed on decks or patios.

Ideally, they should have a lollipop shape. However, rose varieties that tend to cascade or "weep" can also be breathtaking as trees. 'Gourmet Popcorn' grown as a tree graces my own garden and is breathtaking in full bloom. It covers itself with clusters of tiny white blossoms with yellow stamens, surrounded by glossy green foliage.

Insect and disease control can be accomplished more easily with tree roses because the elevation of leaves and blossoms makes it easier to spray underneath where many insects hide.

I like to use non-toxic controls and find that simply hosing off the leaves knocks off the pesky aphids and drowns the spider mites. I've let nature run its course in my garden and now have a balance of beneficial and harmful insects so the insect damage is minimal. As an added benefit, I've observed visiting birds, including Lesser Goldfinch, perch in my roses to feast on insects.

Tree roses differ from shrubs when it comes to pruning. The objective is to enhance their rounded appearance, so pruning is often harsher than on shrubs. At times, it may be necessary to leave twiggy growth to fill in an otherwise barren area to ensure that the tree rose has a well-balanced ball shape. This can result in stems shorter than normally desired for roses used as cut flowers. In cold climates, they're easy to winter-protect by covering the plant with burlap and moving into a garage or storage building.

These are some of my favorite tree roses:

Tall (sixty inches)

'Pillow Fight'—cascading white flowers are fragrant as well as beautiful

'Sea Foam'—weeping white flowers in profusion

'Weeping China Doll'—cascading deep pink flowers

Standard (thirty-six inches)

'Buff Beauty'—fragrant hybrid musk has cascading, soft gold flowers

'Iceberg'—masses of white flowers and bright green leaves

'Gourmet Popcorn'—a real showstopper with tiny white flowers with yellow centers covering the plant in profusion

'Playboy'—vivid, multicolored, orange/yellow single flowers in great abundance

'Perfume Delight' highly fragrant deep pink flowers at nose level

Miniature (eighteen inches)

'Black Jade'—deep dark small red flowers resemble hybrid tea roses

'Little Paradise'—two-tone pink and lavender flowers are very fragrant

'Magic Carrousel'—vibrant red and white flowers in profusion

'Space Odyssey'—single flowers are red with white eye and very dramatic

'Sweet Chariot'—ideal as a tree rose because of cascading growth habit. Very fragrant purple flowers in clusters

Social Climbers

ROSES TO ENJOY IN THE GARDEN, roses to fill vases, and roses to share with friends are the reward of growing climbing roses. One vigorous rose bush, climbing up and outwards to twenty feet, can provide you with hundreds and hundreds of lovely flowers in each bloom cycle. That's why climbing roses are among my favorites. However, there's a price to pay for such lavish production. These are more labor intensive than shrubs or hybrid teas because they require training or staking to supporting structures. There's also more maintenance during the year when it's necessary to deadhead (remove the spent flowers), tie new canes, and continue to train the plant as it grows.

The term "climber" refers to varieties that produce long canes. These can be trained along fences, walls, or arbors. Cane length varies, and can range from eight feet to twenty feet or even larger. Climate also determines size. In general, a rose that behaves as a climber is more vigorous in warmer parts of the nation.

Some of the newer types of shrub roses, such as the David Austin English Roses and the Generosa roses, can also be trained as climbers where I live.

There's a knack to doing this. If the canes are permitted to grow upright, they'll flower only on the ends. But bending the canes horizontally with the growth tip pointing to the ground encourages the plant to produce growth hormones along the length of the cane. Dormant bud eyes grow along the cane and from them will emerge additional canes (called secondary canes). Each one of these is likely to produce a flower. In some varieties, these secondary canes are thick enough to bend and train, and they, too, will produce canes along their lengths that will flower. Talk about flower power!

Many climbing roses produce flowers on old wood, that is, canes that are at least one or two years old. Some don't flower much until they're three years old. It may seem that little is happening to the plant, but actually, it's producing roots to support all the flowers yet to come.

Some, though, bloom on new canes and can be a picture of loveliness from their first year in a garden. One of my favorites is 'Cl. Berries 'n' Cream' for just this reason. Bouquet-like clusters of old rose and cream colored roses are produced in abundance on this remarkable rose. Another variety with the same trait is 'Cl. Fourth of July', a vibrant velvety red striped with bright white. It's the first climber to win the coveted AARS award in twenty-three years.

You can tell that a rose is a climber by its name because it will be designated "Cl." Like other types of roses, climbers are available in a variety of colors, petal shapes and sizes, and fragrances. A wonderful way to enjoy these beauties is on arbors or trellised along a house, especially if they're fragrant and their perfume can waft indoors.

Another trait to look for is strong disease resistance. It's harder to combat those pesky fungal diseases like mildew and rust when the plant covers an entire fence.

The following are some of my favorite climbers, selected for disease resistance and flowering:

'Altissimo'—The very long-lasting single red flowers with yellow stamens have slight fragrance.

'Autumn Sunset'—This pillar-type climber has strong fruity fragrance and apricot-gold color.

'Berries 'n' Cream'—A very free-flowering rose, it has cream clusters with light apple fragrance. It is very disease-resistant.

'Blaze Improved'—The most popular climbing rose since 1932, it has pure red flowers and a light tea scent.

'Don Juan'—The best of the fragrant dark red climbing roses, it has deep velvet-red flowers with a strong rose scent.

'Fourth of July'—Sprays of long-lasting striped red and white flowers on a somewhat smaller plant (ten feet to fourteen feet) have apple fragrance.

'Joseph's Coat'—Multi-colors of red, pink, orange, and yellow appear on a medium-sized plant that is very thorny.

'Pearly Gates'—Pastel pure pink color with strong spice and rose fragrance characterize this new variety (1999).

'Sally Holmes'—This very vigorous plant produces huge clusters of pure white flowers that last and last on the plant and in bouquets. It has slight fragrance but super disease resistance.

'Polka'—Fragrant peach flowers with old-fashioned flower form characterize this moderately sized plant.

making the most of
Miniature Roses

ACENTURY AGO THEY SCARCELY EXISTED. Now, miniature roses are so popular that shoppers can find them for sale in grocery stores where they're being touted as indoor plants. Growing instructions provided with each plant advise buyers to grow them in sunny locations, even indoors in sunny windows. But beware of following this literally. Rose plants belong outdoors, and that includes miniatures. They can always be plugged into a landscape or grown in containers on patios or decks.

I've tried to grow them indoors, and no matter how sunny the location, they invariably grow tall and leggy to try to capture sunlight. Then they suffer from yellowing leaves that drop off. Usually, all the leaves drop off. As soon as I put the pots outdoors, however, they perk right up and continue to grow. If you live in a colder climate, you can grow flowering plants indoors, but you'll have to use special grow lights. The other way you can keep them indoors for decoration is if you treat them as a disposable plant, which is common in Europe where they're sold as disposable indoor floral decoration. But outdoors, they're very versatile and pretty in landscapes in front of borders or any sunny place where you need a one- or two-foot blooming shrub.

Don't be misled by the nomenclature. The formal definition of a miniature rose is one whose flower and foliage is proportionately small. Some varieties can grow as tall as four feet, while others are a petite twelve inches. The most diminutive are called microminis because these tiny plants, such as 'Tom Thumb' and 'Baby Ophelia', reach just six to eight inches with corresponding tiny blooms and foliage. There are even varieties that grow as climbing roses.

Mini roses look like they've been zapped by a futuristic scientist who shrunk a perfectly shaped hybrid tea or floribunda bush into tiny proportions. But they are a natural occurrence in the rose kingdom. They first appeared in 1815 when a variety of Rosa chinensis minima was discovered in Europe. These tiny roses became a very popular fad, but like so many fads, their novelty wore thin over time. Many years later, they were rediscovered by chance when a rose expert noticed some miniature roses growing in a window box in a Swiss village. He got some cuttings of the plant, which the family had been nurturing carefully for almost a century. In the intervening time, these tiny roses have become so popular that hybridizers have created thousands of new varieties. They come in a dazzling array of colors, including the always popular shades of pink, red, and yellow. Buyers can also find them in pure white and novelty colors including oranges, stripes, two-tones, and "hand-painted" roses with colors that bleed and intensify as the blossoms age. Flower forms range from simple singles to classic, high-centered exhibition shapes, and a vast array in between. Many lack fragrance, but some, especially lavender hues, are sweetly scented.

Whatever the variety, all have the same growing needs: abundant sunshine, water, and fertilizer. An easy way to save time and effort is to repot mini rose plants from four-inch containers into fourteen- or sixteen-inch containers, which are often decorative. In days of intense heat or wind, it might be necessary to water containers daily, as is true for most plants. On days with cooler temperatures and cloudy skies, reduce frequency to several times a week.

Mini roses need food, but not as much as their larger relatives. I often use a foliar fertilizer, diluted to one-half the package directions. Mini roses also thrive with fish emulsion, also diluted to one-half the package directions. It's very common to burn foliage and roots of miniature plants, especially if they grow in a garden with other plants, and the gardener fertilizes for the larger shrubs. Avoid using fertilizers that contain systemic insecticides, which will kill miniature rose plants. Instead, to combat unwanted insects, hose off the foliage, especially under leaves where most pests hide. Miniature roses grow on their own roots, so pruning is simple. Many people just cut them back by two-thirds. Prune when the ground has thawed and there's no danger of frost. Minis are the easiest of all roses to prune—you can even use hedge shears.

Some Recommended Miniatures

'Gingerbread Man' apricot

'Jean Kenneally' apricot pink

'Just For You' deep pink with light reverse

'Little Artist' crimson red painted petals with white eye

'Renny' clear pink

'Ring of Fire' orange blend

'Santa Claus' deep red

'Starla' white

'Sequoia Gold' yellow

'Snow Bride' white

'Sugar Plum' mauve

Climbing miniatures

'Candy Cane' striped pink and white

'Hurdy Gurdy' striped red and white

'Jeanne Lajoie' pink

Basic Requirements

YOU CAN GROW ROSES WHEREVER YOU ARE. Whether you own a house with a large yard or rent an apartment with a small deck or balcony, you can enjoy the color and fragrance of roses because there's a rose plant for practically any outdoor situation. Some roses are so small that their flowers are only one-half inch in diameter. The plant size is correspondingly small and grows happily in decorative pots.

Then there are ramblers and climbers that can swallow trees or small buildings. In between are roses for most gardens: Myriad miniatures grow from six inches to four feet ("miniature" refers to the size of the flower rather than the plant); polyanthas; freely flowering floribundas; elegant hybrid teas; modern shrubs from one to six feet; grandifloras that grow proudly tall and produce clusters of flowers on each stem; the hundreds of varieties of Old Garden Roses.

You can plant roses almost any time. In Los Angeles, where I live, bare-root roses go into our gardens in early January. Elsewhere, once the frozen ground becomes soft enough to work, roses can be set out in late spring or early summer. I enjoy the bare-root process because it's economical to buy naked plants and watch with wonder as bare sticks transform into floral showpieces. Before you buy a rose, take a little time to evaluate your own loca-

tion. In general, roses need sunlight, nourishing soil, ample water, and occasional food. They also need to be protected from insects or diseases. You'll find more detailed information on these topics in Part Four: Simple Care. This summary will give you a handy overview.

Sun

Roses grow and flower best when they receive at least six hours of daily sunshine. There are a few varieties that can grow in semi-shade, especially some of the Old Garden Roses, but you'll have fewer problems if you select a sunny location. In very hot climates, rose flowers can burn under intense summer rays, so in these regions, protect them from late afternoon sun by planting them in an area where they receive morning light.

Soil

Ideally, garden soil should be rich with organic matter, called humus. A good indication of soil health is the presence of earthworms. Most urban areas have had so much construction take place that soil has been compressed, removed, or damaged in some way. An investment of a little time and money when you first begin the planting process will pay you back later with healthy, vigorous plants. Whether you're beginning a new garden or planting in an existing landscape, prepare the rose bush's new home by adding planting mix to the hole where it will be placed. When it's planted, cover with more planting mix as a mulch to protect the soil and help with water absorption. Local nurseries and garden centers sell products formulated for specific regions.

If you want to grow roses in containers, buy a commercial potting soil rather than relying on soil from your garden. Commercial mixes are light enough for water to pass through easily and are sterilized so that soil-borne diseases are less likely to attack your plants. Be sure to pick a container large enough for your rose bush when it grows and sends out new roots. One-gallon pots work well with small miniature roses—five-gallon pots are even better. Floribundas, small varieties of shrubs and small OGR varieties (up to three feet tall) can grow in containers, too, if they are five to seven gallons in size. Hybrid tea roses are best when grown in fifteen-gallon containers or in the ground, and climbing roses are the same.

Water

Roses need at least one to two inches of water weekly, depending on temperature and climate. When grown in pots, they need even more because water runs out of the container during watering. If soil is very sandy, water runs through quickly and plants may need more frequent watering. If soil has a high clay content, it holds water, so plants need less. You can tell what you have by watering the plant and observing how long it takes for water to percolate through the top inches. If water sits like a puddle, your soil is very heavy with clay and needs more organic matter in it. If water washes through, it's very sandy and more organic matter will build up the soil structure so that it retains water long enough for plant roots to absorb the life-giving moisture. An easy way to tell if your plant is thirsty is to insert a trowel, stick, or your finger into the soil. If the top inch or so is dry, it's time to water.

Fertilizer

There are two schools of thought—organic versus chemical. I explain this in more detail in Part Four: Simple Care. Basically, the organic school says, "Feed the soil and the plants will get their own nutrition when the right elements are present." The chemical method is to feed the plant directly, either by water-soluble formulation or dry granules. Follow your own philosophical belief here. The important point is that roses are living creatures and need food. There are many different methods of fertilizing. Pick the one that best suits your own philosophy and timetable. You can opt for the most expensive way—a time-release chemical fertilizer that is applied once a year, which can save you a lot of time—or less expensive, more frequent fertilizer applications over the course of the growing season.

Pests and Diseases

If you do a little research first, you'll save yourself a lot of future annoyance. Some roses are just more naturally disease resistant and some are like magnets for annoying problems of mildew, rust, and blackspot. Simplify the process by selecting roses that withstand diseases. Insects are another story. Aphids, spider mites, Japanese beetles, cane borers, and budworms may well attack. I rely on mechanical methods of removing offending pests, and planting gardens with enough diverse plants that natural enemies come into my yard to devour the insect pests. If pests seem to be ruling, I use streams of water or even handpick them to outwit them.

I never thought of myself as an expert gardener. During these past twenty years, I've learned how to grow roses and other ornamental and edible plants, and enjoyed lovely gardens. By following some of these easy methods, you can grow and enjoy beautiful roses, too.

Garden Tools
help get the garden growing right

THE MAXIM "THE RIGHT TOOL TO DO THE JOB RIGHT" is as true in
building and maintaining a garden as it is in building a house. But many
gardeners are likely to buy the cheapest and fewest tools they can get away with, then go
about their gardening chores while grabbing the first implement that's handy. This may be
an inexpensive way to garden, but it can cause frustration, muscle fatigue, and short tem-
pers. Tools were created to serve specific purposes such as tilling the soil to harvest crops or
digging up a new garden bed to grow roses.

Garden tools have changed little over the centuries because they really do the tasks for
which they are designed. The only difference with our modern technology is the prolifera-
tion of ergonomic tools, designed to reduce stress and muscle fatigue. When choosing a
tool, it's important to take into account handle length, tool "heft" (ease with which it can be
lifted), and weight of construction material.

Although the profusion of garden tools can seem overwhelming to budding gardeners,
consider that in the 1930s in Germany, there were more than twelve thousand kinds of
spades alone. But a garden enthusiast need not worry about facing bankruptcy to outfit the
garden shed properly. Why are some tools so expensive? Why not just settle for those found
in garden centers and home improvement superstores? The answer lies in the quality of
construction, the manner in which the tools are forged, the execution of design, and the
quality of wood for the handles. If you're planning to garden for five or more years, it's actually more cost-effective to invest in a few well-made tools such as Felco that will last for
decades.

What tools are essential? If you're a novice, try gardening in a small space first—maybe in containers on a deck or patio or in a small garden plot. These tools will serve your needs:

Trowel
Hand pruning shears, Felco #2
Hand rake
Weeder
Weeding fork
Watering can with rubber rose and brass face for easy cleaning

When gardeners are ready to advance to larger landscapes, add the following:

Steel shovel with solid forged socket
Solid forged steel garden fork
Flat head rake
Collinear hoe
Solid forged garden spade
Five-ply reinforced vinyl hose
Water wand with brass spray lance

Advanced gardeners may also want to get:

Hand pruners, Felco #7 with rotating handle
Holster clip for Felco pruner
Japanese weeder
Folding pruning saw
Long-handled loppers
Singing grass shears (sheep shears) for light trimming and pruning

When buying long-handled tools like forks and spades, consider their size. The handle should come to your elbow, when you're standing. The tool should also feel comfortable to hold.

Ratchet pruners are handy for people who experience discomfort when using conventional pruning shears, because they cut through very hard wood with a clickity-clickity-click-pop action. This four-part movement is easier on hands and wrists, especially if there's a lot of pruning to be done.

Maintaining tools is just as important as their selection. Take care to sharpen pruners, shovels, spades, and the like regularly. Oil wooden handles. And of course, a careful gardener never puts a tool away while dirt still clings to the implement.

Like a fine friend, a fine tool just gets better and better over time.

Know Your Soil

PEOPLE WHO GROW CROPS FOR A LIVING take soil science seriously. From strawberries to strawflowers, from corn to Christmas trees, success with plants starts from the ground up. Home gardeners will have healthier plants and enjoy the results of their gardens by paying attention to the health and condition of the soil in which they grow. Roses, while easy to grow in various conditions, thrive when they can spread their roots into fertile, loamy soil containing microorganisms, nutrients, minerals, oxygen, and water. They'll respond to these conditions with vigor and produce larger and better-formed flowers.

It's rare to find perfect soil. Loam is ideal—soil with loads of organic matter, some amount of sand, and enough clay to provide solid anchorage for plants. Too much clay results in hard soil that tends to cake, making it hard for roots to penetrate. If your soil sticks to your shovel, becomes rock hard, or doesn't easily absorb water, you have soil with more clay than sand. Sandy soils contain large particles that won't clump together. The plus side is that it's easy to work. But the openness of the particles allows water to penetrate so quickly that roots can't absorb an adequate amount of water. There's also the problem of fertility. Sandy soil doesn't contain enough nutrients to support roses and many other plants.

The type of soil you have depends on where you live. In my garden, I've experienced clay soil as well as sandy. At one house, I was really fortunate to have inherited a garden with very fertile loamy soil. I suspect that previous owners had diligently worked and amended the soil over a long period of time.

If no one else has done it for you, you'll need to prepare the soil in which you want to grow your roses. You can tell if your soil is fertile by the color. Fertile soils are dark because they contain a lot of organic matter, such as decomposed leaves, which turn into humus after they decay. Humus is a form of organic matter.

In addition to leaf mold, other types of humus include compost, composted steer or chicken manure, and ground peat. Adding copious amounts of humus to your soil will reward you when the roses respond with healthy, green leaves, lots of flowers, and increased resistance to diseases and pests.

There's another factor affecting roses that's called pH. This refers to soil's acidity or alkalinity. Soil pH is measured on a scale of zero to fourteen. Seven is neutral, below seven is acidic and above seven is alkaline. Roses perform best in slightly acidic soil, ranging from 5.8 to 6.8. You can have your soil tested by a professional laboratory, which is the most precise method, or you can buy a do-it-yourself kit sold through nurseries and garden centers. There are even meters available that probe into your soil to give you a fairly accurate idea of your soil's pH. You can change the pH by adding sulfur if the soil is alkaline or ground limestone if the soil is too acidic. However, your water source will also influence soil pH so you should retest your soil every few years. If all this seems too complicated, you can insure the health of your soil and roses by using a lot of organic amendments.

You can add commercial planting mixes and mulches that are available at nurseries and garden centers to your garden in several ways. The easiest is to add planting mix to the hole you dig when you plant your rose bush. Combine equal parts mix with the native soil, plant the bush, fill the hole, and spread the remaining mixture over the surface as mulch.

When I start a new garden, I prefer to rototill large amounts of planting mix into the soil. When I recently moved to a hillside home, I removed the existing ice plant and few trees, brought in twelve cubic yards of planting mix, and rototilled it into the level sections of the property. The ground is heavy clay, so even with all this amendment, I still add more mix to each planting hole. After the roses were planted, I spread more on top of the soil to act as mulch, which over the course of the gardening year will decompose into the soil. Sometimes it takes several years of faithfully amending and mulching a garden before the soil is really rich and healthy. During the process, positive changes are taking place underground. In just three months, earthworms have moved in. When I first worked the soil, no living creatures could be found. Soon, millions of microscopic soil microorganisms will take up residence to further enhance soil and plant vitality. Soil is about more than dirt.

Bare-Root Roses

THE MOST COST-EFFECTIVE WAY TO BUY ROSES is when they are in the condition called bare-root. These roses have no soil around the roots, making them lighter for shipping and easy to plant. Most of America's forty million rose bushes are dug, sorted, and stored for delivery to nurseries according to regional planting time once a year, in fall. Mail-order nurseries ship plants in the bare-root stage from January through May so they arrive at the destination according to proper planting time for the location.

I prefer to buy roses bare-root because they're less costly than canned bushes (the fertilizer, water, and labor involved in growing potted plants throughout the year are paid for by the customer), and more important, I can see the plant's roots.

Length and quantity of rose roots are vital for vigorous plants. A rose bush trying to survive with puny roots is usually weak and produces small quantities of inferior blooms. So, I avoid buying roses in packages and instead choose from the hundreds of varieties offered at local nurseries where plants are stored in bins filled with a sawdust mixture. This enables me to observe every part of the plant before I make my selection.

A rose plant can live for fifty years or more, so it's a good investment of time and money to select the best possible plant. Bare-root roses are graded according to federal standards, and this is the first helpful criterion to use in making a selection. Plants with three or more canes are Grade Number 1. Plants with at least two canes are Grade Number 1½, and Grade Number 2 plants have only one cane. It's best to select only Grade Number 1. Avoid the temptation to select a cheaper grade because the resulting plant performance is usually disappointing. Most top nurseries only stock Grade Number 1.

Look for plants with large, thick canes, but keep in mind that different rose varieties

have different types of canes. Generally, hybrid tea roses produce large canes, while flori-bunda and shrub roses can have a multitude of pencil-thin canes.

If a plant you select has canes that are longer than its roots, even out the plant by removing the extra cane length. The proportion of root to cane must be in balance for the plant to thrive. (If the roots are longer than the canes, buy the plant and rejoice). Inspect the roots carefully and try to avoid plants with broken roots.

If you understand the different parts of a rose plant, you'll be better able to care for the plant. From ground up, here's a simple description:

Rootstock or understock—Approximately seventy-five percent of all roses grown commercially are budded onto a different rose variety. In most cases, 'Dr. Huey' is preferred, but roses shipped to eastern states are frequently budded onto different varieties that better withstand cold temperatures. Since 1995, however, there's an increasingly strong trend toward growing roses on their own roots—now an estimated twenty-five percent of all roses are grown directly on their own roots.

Bud union or crown—Those roses that are grafted have a bud union, the graft where a length of bud wood from the intended plant will grow and from which the desired flower canes will emerge. Grafted roses are usually grown in fields for two years before they're harvested and sold. This allows time for the desired plant to mature.

Canes—The source of flowers.

Suckers—Canes that the understock can send up above ground. You can identify a sucker because the leaves are shaped differently from the plant growing from the bud union and if allowed to flower, they're usually red (like 'Dr. Huey'). Remove suckers from under the ground as close to their growing source as possible.

Basal breaks—A very desirable new cane emerging from the bud union. You can identify it first as a red spot on the bud union that gradually swells as it matures into a large, thick cane. This is the way budded rose plants produce new canes to sustain the plant.

Corolla—The technical term for the rose flower.

Sepals—The green outer petals that protect the developing flower bud. They drop down as the flower opens.

Calyx—The swollen part immediately under the flower.

Peduncle—The thin stem immediately beneath the calyx.

Own-Root Roses

Increasingly, roses on their own roots are replacing grafted roses, for several reasons.

This is a more cost-effective method and can help growers get their roses into the marketplace more quickly, especially in the case of miniature roses, which can be sold when they're one year old or younger.

Own-root roses are hardier in climates that experience winter freeze because the roots below ground will send up new growth in spring.

Own-root roses don't produce suckers.

Some rose experts say own-root roses are stronger and live longer than grafted roses.

Planting Your Roses

WHETHER YOU BUY YOUR BARE-ROOT ROSE at a nursery or obtain it through a mail-order source, here are some tips for ensuring that the plant will grow and thrive for years to come.

Planting a Bare-Root Rose

Soak the plant in water for at least twenty-four hours. I fill a large trash can and immerse the plant or plants so even the canes are covered. This thorough soaking enables drying roots or canes to rehydrate. Some rosarians recommend adding some vitamin B1 (sold at all nurseries) to give the plant a boost.

Be sure to dig a proper hole at least eighteen inches deep and two feet across to give those all-important roots plenty of room.

I like to add some bonemeal and pure alfalfa meal in the bottom of the planting hole. Alfalfa boosts roses because it has hormones that promote vigorous growth. I buy alfalfa meal in fifty-pound sacks at a feed store and give all my roses an alfalfa feed in January or February.

Add some organic planting mix and blend well with the garden soil.

Make a mound at the bottom of the hole and place the rose on it. Gently spread the roots so they drape over the mound. The hole should be large enough so that the roots aren't crowded. In frost-free regions, the plant should be an inch or two higher than the soil level once in place. In colder climates, position the bud union several inches below soil level to protect it in future winters.

After you've positioned the plant, gently fill the hole with a mixture of planting mix and soil.

Mound leftover soil to form a basin around the rose for ease of watering. Fill the basin at least twice so water deeply penetrates the soil. Then place extra potting mix around the plant to serve as mulch.

Cover the canes with a very large plastic bag or mound planting mix to prevent them from drying out if desiccating winds howl through the region. Gently uncover them when new growth emerges along the canes. Wait until the new growth is at least two inches before fertilizing, usually a month or so after planting.

Planting a Potted Rose

When roses are already producing leaves or flowers, use a different method.

Dig a hole at least as deep and wide as a five-gallon container. If the container is one gallon, dig the hole slightly wider but not deeper. You can use the shovel handle as a measuring guide while digging the hole.

Place soil amendment, such as alfalfa meal, at bottom of hole, then cover with a thin layer of soil.

Tip container on side and gently remove plant without disturbing root ball. If the plant doesn't move easily, cut the container off with sharp shears. Again, be careful not to disturb the root ball.

Position plant in hole and gently fill in with extra soil. Use extra soil or planting mix to cover area as mulch.

Tamp soil and create a watering basin surrounding the plant.

Water deeply.

If you want to grow climbing roses, plant them where you can support the long canes that will emerge in time. Use a fence, wall, or trellis and when long canes emerge in a year or two, tie them with a garden tie against the support. Be sure to bend the long cane to a horizontal position as this will encourage additional canes to emerge from the horizontal ones in the future. This gives maximum flower production.

When to Water

ALTHOUGH ROSES NEED WATER, they don't like excessive amounts. Too much, especially in heavy or clay soil, can cause serious problems. If water doesn't drain well, which is what happens in clay soil, the root ball can be immersed in the wet stuff to the point where root rot may develop. If unnoticed, the plant can die. Another circumstance when this can happen is if the rose bush is planted in an area where water accumulates. Perhaps it's the low point of a garden. Perhaps drains lead to the site. Or maybe sprinklers are too heavy at one particular section. Any of these conditions can hurt the rose bush. Lack of sufficient water also brings on problems when plants don't receive enough to support their leaves and flowers. An easy way to tell when this happens is if new growth wilts.

In general, mature rose bushes require at least one inch of water each week. Experienced gardeners can tell from leaf color and texture if the plant needs water. Another symptom of water problems is yellowing of the leaves. However, this happens when roses are overwatered as well as underwatered. The best way to tell is by checking the soil either with your hand or a probe. If the top few inches of soil are dry, it's time to irrigate. Water requirements vary by season and location. In regions of the country that receive abundant

rainfall, gardeners can usually rely on nature to do the watering. In arid regions, some type of watering system is needed.

For gardeners who grow just a few roses, whether in the landscape or in containers, applying water with a watering can or hose can do the job. Plan on watering once or twice a week, depending on temperatures and wind conditions. Be sure to give enough water that it penetrates eighteen inches into the soil. If you have more than six or so roses, you might prefer to invest in a watering system.

Some gardeners like drip irrigation systems as an efficient way to get water to the plant roots. The ground-level irrigation system ensures that no water is lost to wind, runoff, or evaporation. However, my experience has been that unless this type of system is thoroughly checked frequently, problems may go unnoticed until the plant is in severe distress, perhaps even dies. Tiny emitter lines can clog with soil particles or mineral salts in some areas. Mechanical disturbance from animals or accidental gardening mishaps can also go undetected.

I've had success with soaker hoses set out in defined garden beds to form a perimeter line. These devices emit water through tiny holes along the entire hose, and the water percolates down to the roots without any loss of moisture. It's a simple and inexpensive solution.

Another easy way to get water to your roses is with a hose-end attachment. Some are on stakes that can be positioned into the ground in the region where you need to water. Another type is called a bubbler because the water does just that. It bubbles out of the device at a low enough pressure to soak the area and with minimal water loss into the air. If you choose to use a bubbler, be sure to build a basin around the rose bush so water remains in the root zone.

An automated irrigation system is a long-term investment that can actually save time, effort, and aggravation over the long run. There are various types of sprinkler systems as well as drip irrigation or hybrid micro-mister versions. If you're the do-it-yourself type of person, you can get supplies and instructions from local nurseries and garden centers. I'm not too handy, so I opted to have an irrigation specialist install my system. Because the garden is large and has different exposures and conditions, the system is designed as a series of stations so that water delivery can be adjusted for time and quantity, depending on the specific needs of the garden location.

If your plant is growing in a container, water several times consecutively and really drench the pot. If the rootball has dried out, water can run along the sides of the container without adequately penetrating the root area. Several repeated water flushes avoids this problem. Early morning is the best time to water, especially if you use a sprinkler system. This gives plants a chance to store water before the heat of the day and also allows foliage to dry off before evening. There's a misunderstanding about water on leaves and fungal diseases. A rose myth is that watering leaves leads to mildew and blackspot. The conventional wisdom has been never to wet rose leaves, but I've checked with rose experts who debunk this theory. Washing off leaves is actually good for the plants because it removes insects and disease spores.

If you have any questions about what's best for your situation, check with experts in your area at your public garden or nursery.

When to Feed

I'M ALWAYS AMAZED WHEN PEOPLE tell me that their roses don't grow or bloom for them. They go on to tell me that they're helpless at growing roses. When I ask when was the last time they fed their rose bushes, they often look surprised and reply, "Oh, do roses need food?"

People feed their pets because the animals bark, meow, screech, or in some way tell us they are hungry. Unfortunately, plants lack a vocal method of communicating to us. But they are living creatures, and need food. When roses grow in the wild, as species roses have done for more than five million years, they can find their own food by sending roots out into nutritious soil. Sadly, when humans build their habitats, they've usually altered the soil and environment so that it lacks many of the elements necessary for plants to sustain themselves. Humans have to lend a helping hand. Often.

Roses have an undeserved reputation of being demanding plants that need a lot of care to flourish and flower. This is nonsense. All it takes is a little understanding of their basic needs. You can grow roses that reward you with loads of flowers if you just take a little time to feed them. The timetable varies on your location. In general, begin fertilization when the new spring growth is about two-inches long. You can feed a few times during the gardening season, or more often if you want more flowers.

In general, fertilize in spring and summer, and stop before frosts can come. I begin feeding in late March when most of my roses are vigorously sending out new growth. Another feeding in late spring carries them to summer. Then, because temperatures soar above one hundred degrees, I stop until late summer. Another round of fertilizer in fall means I can pick roses in December.

There are various ways to fertilize. The most expensive, but easiest, is to use time-release fertilizer once a year. The protective coating breaks down as soil and temperatures warm. This means you don't have to think about feeding the plants again for the year.

I prefer to interact with my roses and like to feed more frequently. I scatter granules around the garden and then water them in. Another easy method is with water-soluble fertilizers that can be used while watering the roses. If you want dramatic results, use a diluted solution, at one-half the recommended strength, twice as often. This gives the plants a steady supply of nutrients, which is especially helpful if you grow your roses in containers.

Every serious rose gardener seems to have a special formula or recipe for success.

Like cooks who add their personal touch to cherished recipes, these rose growers get very enthusiastic about their special fertilizer formulas. Don't let this deter you from growing roses. Roses are very tough, very forgiving plants that will flower readily, even with just a little tender loving care. One of my favorite stories that proves this is told by Tom Carruth. He had created a rose garden containing three hundred rose bushes. When he bought another house in a nearby city, a friend looked after the rose garden while the house was for sale. It took more than a year for the house to sell. During that time, the roses received water because they were on an automated system. But they weren't fertilized for the entire year. Tom was very surprised to see that those roses bloomed as well and as much as the roses in his new garden, which he had faithfully fertilized throughout the year.

The message here is that roses are indeed tough plants. However, it doesn't mean you shouldn't fertilize your roses at all. That rose garden had received quite a bit of fertilizer over the years and the soil was filled with nutrients which over a long period of time will become depleted. By all means, feed those rose bushes, but don't feel overwhelmed.

"Basal Breaks"

It's not an old wives' tale. Epsom salts scattered around the base of roses really does contribute to new canes coming out of the plant base. These are called "basal breaks." Use a large handful for mature rose plants and a few teaspoons for year-old bushes or miniature rose plants.

Fertilizing

organic or chemical?

THERE ARE TWO SCHOOLS OF THOUGHT about feeding flowers and plants. The organic approach in effect feeds the soil by providing nutrients obtained through organic matter like aged manure, fish emulsion, blood meal, and other natural sources. Microorganisms in healthy soil break these materials down into the nitrogen, phosphorus, and potassium (NPK) required by plants. Plant roots absorb them as needed, along with a host of micronutrients.

The conventional approach advocates the use of fertilizers formulated from chemicals and containing the NPK and trace elements absorbed by plants. I've listened to expert gardeners who say that plants don't know or care if their nutrition comes from chemical laboratories or microorganisms, as long as they get adequate nutrition. I have a friend who is a trained chemist and has a natural green thumb. He uses diluted amounts of a chemical fertilizer each time he waters his plants, and has very healthy plants that produce loads of flowers. But detractors of the conventional chemical approach deride these fertilizers as "junk food" for plants that can give them the equivalent of a sugar high.

Organic Gardening Magazine published a study several years ago comparing several plants fed solely with organic fertilizers and the equivalent plants fed with a popular water-soluble fertilizer that's usually applied with a hose-end sprayer. For the first few years, the chemical fertilizer had more significant results. The organic method kicked in after three years, and by the seventh year, plants fed with the chemical fertilizer were weak and puny, while their organically raised counterparts thrived. The moral I derived is that the method depends on your motives. If you want instant results, without thought of long-term effects, use the chemical fertilizers, which are known for ease of application. If you're concerned about fertilizer runoff that might contaminate oceans, groundwater, and surrounding soil, and you have a long-term investment in your property, organic fertilizers are for you.

I hedge my bets and do both. I use a granular fertilizer every spring and fall, and in between I use rose food formulated with organic matter including aged chicken manure, bat guano, kelp, and alfalfa. I also cover the garden surface with cocoa bean mulch because I love its deep brown appearance (and yes, I admit I love the sweet chocolate scent that wafts into my house for several weeks after the mulch is applied). My time is very limited and this way I feel that I'm providing excellent nutrition for my plants without feeling as though I'm a slave to my garden or creating untold harm to the surrounding environment.

I also know gardeners who simply use a water-soluble fertilizer once a month. When I first started growing roses in 1983, I used that method, too. But after several years, I noticed that the rose bushes weren't thriving. I did try the all-organic method, but wasn't satisfied with the results—too few blossoms for my purposes. However, to be fair to organic gardeners, if you invest several years and can spend the time to apply the manure teas, alfalfa meal, fish meal, and other organic ingredients, you will have spectacular results.

The most important point is that roses do need to be fed. Your time and interest will be the factors that determine which method to use. Roses love tea and coffee. Toss your coffee grounds and old tea leaves around the base of the bushes. Before you use any fertilizer, be sure that the bushes have been thoroughly watered so they can absorb the fertilizer. Follow package directions carefully to prevent burning leaves, as some chemical fertilizers can burn if they are applied to dry plants or in too strong a concentration.

Whichever method you prefer, feed those roses and enjoy beautiful bouquets in the months to come.

Tea Time

Roses like tea and coffee. Save those old tea bags, tea leaves, and coffee grounds for the rose bushes. Scatter around the base of each bush for a pick-me-up for the garden.

Confessions
of a reformed pesticide junky

ONCE UPON A TIME, my garage shelves contained unpronounceable chemical insecticides and fungicides whose bottles listed dire warnings to users. Now, a lone half-empty bottle of insecticidal soap sits alongside a box of neem oil.

My early training was by ardent and overly enthusiastic rosarians who combat the endless onslaught of leaf-chewing, bud-destroying, stem-sucking insects whose only mission in life seemed that of disfiguring flower gardens. Rosarians exhibit their prize blooms in shows where not even a ragged leaf or torn flower petal is permissible, making them among the most aggressive attackers of all insect life.

When I planted a dozen rose bushes in 1983 and sought the advice of expert rosarians, they told me that my garden equipment had to include power sprayers, an array of insecticides, miticides, and fungicides, and, of course, protective gear for me, the human who applied these chemicals faithfully every week from spring through fall.

Although my motivation was to enjoy the blooms on the bushes in my garden and in vases throughout my home, I, too, wanted perfect roses and was willing to do what conventional wisdom deemed necessary. So, I dutifully sprayed, misted, spritzed, and fogged. As newer and more potent products came onto the market, I eagerly added them to my growing chemical arsenal.

A few years of this practice indeed resulted in a pest-free garden. I was bewildered at the dismay of a fellow gardening enthusiast who was sure my life was in dire danger by applying these chemicals. "Nonsense," I protested. "Everybody else is doing it. And I'm only spraying an hour or so a week. I'm sure that's not harming me."

My attitude and gardening practice changed the summer day I was aggressively attacking fleas. I was using a malathion-based product I'd bought at a pet store. Happily envisioning flea-free cats, I conscientiously sprayed the lawn very thoroughly. A breeze came up and wafted the spray in my face, teaching me why spraying is not done on a breezy day. Waves of nausea and dizziness coursed through me. I dropped the equipment and staggered inside. I envisioned the ambulance racing through my neighborhood to transport my almost lifeless body to the hospital, but fortunately the nausea and dizziness eased after twenty or thirty minutes.

"Hmm," I thought. "Maybe I'm allergic to malathion. I'd better stay away from that one."

Several months later in 1989, Los Angeles embarked on the controversial aerial spraying of malathion in an all-out effort to stop the fruit fly infestation that was threatening the agricultural industry. I, along with other enraged and alarmed citizens, vocally protested the aerial helicopter drops. Even so, I knew that the alarm was highly exaggerated—after all, home gardeners use a much greater concentration of the chemical in the privacy of their own yards. I began to feel like a hypocrite. How could I protest the actions of the city officials when I was guilty of much greater pesticide mania?

I started to watch my garden more closely. In spring, I saw migrating bushtits perching in the rose bushes feasting on the aphids and green lacewings that had been feasting on the aphids, too. That was the spring I'd been lazy and used a systemic fertilizer and insecticide. With sudden horror, I realized that the birds were probably consuming toxic bugs containing lethal poisons that would kill them, too.

That did it for me. I turned in the poisons and my "nuclear bomb" approach to pest control for the saner, safer non-toxic method.

It took a year of self-control to avoid the temptation to run for the poison blasts when the first colonies of spring aphids appeared. I began to tolerate thrips in the rose blossoms. I stopped regarding spiders as loathsome and valued them for their greedy appetites for thrips, spider mites, and aphids. I no longer shuddered when the wasps flew around my roses, for I learned that they were feasting on thrips. I began to value blasts of water, soapy solutions, and even letting Nature take her course.

"It's absurd that insects shouldn't be in gardens," says Mike Atkins, Ph.D., one of the nation's most respected entomologists and a founder of the Safer non-toxic products for pest control. He and other experts who advocate a safe and sane approach to gardening point out that nature has a way of balancing pests and predators if humans will not interfere.

It becomes a matter of deciding how much plant damage the gardener is willing to tolerate. I've learned to tolerate a great deal. In the last few years, I've only resorted to soap sprays a few times, in early spring. Instead, I import ladybugs, green lacewings, and syrphid flies, all with voracious appetites for the bugs I don't want in my garden—aphids, spider mites, and thrips. Now, I applaud each and every spider in my garden, and when I accidentally transport some into my house after I've cut flowers for my vases, I carefully catch the spider on a leaf and put it back where it can do its duty. This is a radical change from my childhood growing up in New York City, where I thought that the only good bug was a dead one.

I'm still battling ants, however, for they are among the worst pests in a garden. Ants colonize aphids and scale for their honeydew and also spread a sooty mold. To their credit, ants eat termites and fleas, and I've noticed a decrease in the flea population.

I'm now practicing what the experts who preach Integrated Pest Management (IPM) recommend. IPM is an ecologically balanced approach to pest management. Instead of using chemicals as a first line of defense, they become a last resort. IPM is a numbers game. You determine the number of pests you're willing to tolerate (zero for a rose exhibitor, considerably more for a garden hobbyist). I'm now willing to put up with minor "bad" insect damage in exchange for peace of mind and body, so it works for me.

I have a clear conscience now as flocks of birds enter my garden. I know my cats who love to lounge among the rose bushes aren't at risk. But I also experienced a poignant reminder of the damage caused by our attempts to control the environment. I found a Great Horned Owl in obvious distress. He was so weak that he didn't attempt to move or even lift his head. I rushed him to a friend, a licensed wild bird rehabilitator, who placed him in a temperature-controlled incubator and administered subcutaneous fluids, tube feedings, and special medicine. The owl was a victim of poison—probably from ingesting a mouse or rat. This magnificent bird died needlessly, and he's only one of the many hundreds and thousands of birds victimized by mankind's poisons.

We may feel powerless to change the world, but we certainly can change our actions in the habitat and portion of planet Earth that we do control—our own gardens.

I'm glad I did.

Garlic is said to banish evil spirits and can also keep insects away. Try one of the garlic-based insecticides now available in nurseries.

Prepare Your Roses
for summer's heat

WHEN SPRING MAKES WAY FOR SIZZLING SUMMER, you can see the difference in your garden wherever you live. Expect the size of rose blossoms to diminish when soaring temperatures stress the bushes. Fragrance dissipates in the hot breezes, and red roses quickly crimp and burn. But don't despair. Roses are tough plants. A little tender loving care will help them through the dog days of summer and enable them to bounce back with a brilliant display of fall blossoms in regions where Septembers are frost-free.

One of the most important ways to help your roses (and all your garden plants) is by mulching the soil. Spread homemade, well-aged compost, commercial soil amendment—even straw or newspaper—on top of the garden soil in a layer at least three to four inches thick. Cover the exposed soil, but be sure the mulch is at least six inches away from the bud union at the base of the plant so that insects won't attack the region.

Mulching retains water in the soil, cools soil temperature, and has the added benefit of reducing weed growth. You'll discover that you won't need to water your plants as often because soil won't dry out as fast.

If you live in a region that doesn't experience summer rains, you'll need to irrigate your roses. Be sure to soak each plant deeply. Avoid the temptation of sprinkling the surface with a hose. Water should penetrate to a depth of twelve inches to encourage the plants to send their roots deeper into the soil for their moisture and nourishment. The time it takes to do this varies in each garden. Type of soil, sun exposure, and sloping property all have an effect. When I first established my rose gardens, I probed into the soil with a trowel to find

out how deeply the water had penetrated right after I had turned on the sprinklers. Now I know that I need to water for fifteen or twenty minutes in summer, three times a week (every other day when the hot Santa Ana winds suck moisture from the foliage.)

Summer is also the time to stop feeding the rose bushes. They're putting enough energy into combating one-hundred-degree-plus temperatures and don't need to be forced to bloom at a time of year when it's not easy for them. In frost-free regions, wait until mid-September, when cooler days are in sight, to apply fertilizer. You'll find that some varieties will continue to produce blossoms, and they'll do fine on the nutrients already in the ground.

Winter Care

THE EASIEST WAY TO ENSURE THAT YOUR ROSES will survive harsh winters is to plant roses developed especially for cold climates. Explorer, Buck, and Parkland are three excellent series developed in Canada and the United States especially for areas where winters are severe. Because they were developed from certain types of species roses growing naturally in harsh regions, these cold-hardy roses will thrive will little special care. When winter comes, just follow a few steps and these hardy roses will make it through harsh winters without major problems. Christian Bédard grew roses in the Quebec area before moving to sunny Southern California to join the staff at Weeks Roses. He safeguarded his Explorer roses by tying canes together with strong string and then covering each rose bush with a commercial rose protection device called a snow fence. Made of wire and wood, it forms a protective barrier around the plant so branches can't break off in snow or ice storms.

If you want to grow hybrid tea or other types of tender roses, you'll need to give them a little more care to protect them if you live in regions where temperatures drop to fifteen degrees Fahrenheit or less. First, in late fall, prune canes to a length of eight to ten inches. Wait until a few weeks of below-freezing temperatures have occurred before protecting them because roses need a brief time to adjust to the colder temperatures. This is called "hardening off." Once this has occurred, cover the base of the plant with mulch. If you have just a few roses, protect each one with a commercial rose cone for insulation and secure the cones with a brick. If the rose cone lacks air holes, punch in some so that humidity doesn't build up in fall or early spring. Snow will insulate and protect rose bushes when they're dormant in winter, but excessive moisture can harm the canes. If you have a large rose garden, you can protect the bushes with a commercial rose blanket that can be supported on stakes

and fastened around a large area. Check with your local nursery for their availability.

Climbing roses and tree roses call for a different wintering technique. Untie climbing roses from their supports, lay the canes on the ground, and cover them with mulch. For tree roses, partially dig them out of the ground, lean them over so that they lie on or near the ground, and cover them with mulch or a similar insulating material.

In early spring, remove the cone approximately one month before freezing temperatures are expected to end. Remove some of the mulch material without exposing the base. After a few weeks, once the roses have adapted to the weather, remove the remaining mulch. Prune off any dead wood from the canes (it'll look black) and in a short time, dormant buds will swell, turn red, and new growth will emerge. Begin fertilizing when new growth is several inches long. You can find Explorer, Buck, and Parkland roses in nurseries or specialty rose companies.

Be especially respectful of roses in fall and winter, when their thorns become brittle.

Arm Yourself
and prune those roses

IF YOU REGARD PRUNING ROSES WITH DREAD, you might find it comforting to think of yourself as a sculptor who is fashioning a new and more attractive statue. Only yours is a living plant.

In warm regions, January and February are the months to prune roses. Every year, when I sharpen my pruning shears and don gear to protect me from wicked thorns, I always wonder what insanity came over me when I filled my garden with roses from ground to tree level. With more than one hundred roses of various varieties, from tiny miniatures to sprawling climbing roses that reach twenty feet, I sometimes think it would have been easier if I had fallen in love with daylilies, daisies, or perennials that go dormant and die back all by themselves. I wouldn't have to work so hard and long to reshape all these plants. Yet with the first flush of spring bloom, I'm intoxicated again with the Queen of Flowers.

Over the years, I've learned a few techniques to speed up the process and make it more enjoyable.

1. **Arm yourself with the best tools you can buy.** There's a reason that Felco, Fiskars, and other top-quality pruning shears and loppers are costly. They're well designed and help reduce muscle fatigue. This is very important when you're pruning dozens of bushes in a single day. Be sure that they are very sharp. I have mine professionally sharpened every January so they make quick, smooth cuts right where I want them. You will need several different types of pruners. Use a classic bypass pruning shear for most floribunda and hybrid tea roses. Keep a tool belt or container for

your shears so that you don't lose them in the midst of leaves or canes while you're working. Thick canes require a heftier tool, and that's when you need to reach for loppers. The extra handle length provides better leverage. Some canes can grow so thick that you need to remove them with a pruning saw. Some dedicated rose fanciers use bonsai tools or scissors to prune miniature roses. But if you're not exhibiting them, you can save time by shearing mini roses at ground level to remove all upper growth. They're growing on their own roots and will shoot out new canes with a flourish.

2. **Protect yourself.** Wear durable gloves, preferably with gauntlets to protect your arms. I tend to avoid gloves because I like the feel of soil, flowers, and tools in my hands. But a session with a climbing rose changed my attitude. One year I was pruning 'Cl. Dortmund', a vigorous red-flowered climber renowned for wicked thorns. I was trying to do the job in a short-sleeved shirt and no gloves. I perse-

vered but realized I was foolish when a friend asked if I had been in a car accident because of all the deep scratches on my arms. During winter dormancy, canes are stiffer, and thorns are dried out and more lethal.

3. **To help your roses prepare** for a new year of luxuriant blooms, you generally need to remove one-third to one-half of the previous year's growth.

4. **Cut away dead canes,** crossing canes, and weak, spindly growth that won't produce any worthwhile flowers.

5. **Remove all leaves and cart them away.** They can harbor disease spores such as rust or mildew.

6. **It's a good practice to dip your shears in a bleach solution** (two tablespoons to a quart of water; wipe shears after dipping) to prevent transmitting rose diseases from bush to bush.

7. **Seal cut canes with nail polish,** glue, or a commercial rose pruning sealant so that borers can't enter.

8. **Complete the pruning by cleaning up** any weeds growing around the roses.

9. **Add a large handful of Epsom salts** at the base of each bush. This helps encourage basal breaks, healthy new canes that emerge from the bud union.

10. **If you haven't yet mulched your roses, now is the time.** Don't fertilize the bushes until the new growth is at least two inches long.

Prune most roses in late fall just before you place a protective covering over them for the winter. Prune canes to eight to twelve inches in length. In spring, you'll need to prune again to remove canes damaged by dieback during winter. Cut away these black canes to living tissue, which is soft and green. Remove weak or crossing canes.

Shrub roses don't need severe pruning; shape and open the center for good air circulation. Tree roses should be pruned to form a compact round ball. Dead canes should be removed, too.

In warm climates, roses that grow tall or sprawl will benefit from a light shaping in summer. Remove up to one-third of the plant's growth. Be sure to keep lots of leaves to help the bush withstand sizzling sun and torrid temperatures. If you're like me, you'll be pruning your rose bushes each time you cut off a flower for indoor enjoyment. This is the simplest way to keep roses in good shape and attractive form.

Caring for Shrubs

SHRUB ROSES ARE THE NEW KIDS ON THE BLOCK. Rose companies are promoting varieties like 'Carefree Delight', 'Carefree Wonder', 'Knock Out', 'Simplicity', and others as easy-care landscape plants that give loads of lovely flowers for very little effort on the gardener's part. The claim is true, although the definition is a little misleading. All rose plants are shrubs by definition—they're woody plants that can live for many years, like lilacs or forsythias. The current term is more of a definition by usage—roses in landscapes that are free-flowering, very disease-resistant, cold-hardy, and grow well among other plants.

Shrub roses are bred and selected more for their landscape qualities as an overall plant than for their flower form. In the twentieth century, hybrid teas commanded center stage and dominated the rose market. That's changing now as more and more gardeners want colorful, fragrant, abundantly flowering roses that are attractive plants, too.

Breeders are responding with many choices. David Austin was a trailblazer when he developed his English roses, a happy marriage of old rose form and fragrance on plants that are attractive in landscapes. However, some of the varieties are notorious for disease problems. As Austin's varieties became more widely accepted, other breeders around the world also concentrated on producing shrub roses with great results. Now rose lovers can select from the Towne & Country series, the Carefree series, the Meidiland series, hybrid rugosas, Modern Antiques, and Shrublets.

Their compact size means they can highlight flower borders, double as landscape hedges the way 'Simplicity' does, and form the foundation for old-fashioned cottage gardens in small urban areas. Modern shrub roses tend to be more compact than antique roses that can swallow a lot of garden space. Today's gardens are considerably smaller than those of a

century or two ago, so space is usually at a premium.

Caring for shrubs is simple. Plant them in sunny locations, water deeply, and fertilize occasionally. Diseases are rarely a problem. Prune only to shape by removing dead or spindly canes, but don't remove too much growth. Some varieties produce roses on stems too short for cutting. You can leave them on the bushes to enjoy in the garden or cut blossoms to float in water.

Going Buggy

PUT IN A PLANT AND THEY WILL COME—the bugs, that is. Tiny flying gnats, slithering snails, microscopic mites, and a lot more. There's a jungle out there in your garden. But if you think, as I first did, that the only good bug is a dead bug, please reconsider. Nature is filled with contrasts and it really is a bug-eat-bug world, especially in a garden. The trick is to know which bugs you want and which exist solely to devour or disfigure your roses.

This takes a little work on the part of the gardener. When you notice that the rose leaves have emerged and the flower buds are forming, you can be sure there's a lot of insect activity occurring, too. Take a close look at your plant before you rush out and spray everything in sight with the latest insecticide. If you plan your strategy, you really won't have to wage an insect war at all. Nature will do it for you. There are several ways you can help the process.

Don't spray toxic insecticides. They'll kill the beneficials as well as the pests.

Do include plants in the landscape that will attract the good bugs, either through their nectar or their pollen. Here are some of their favorites:

Baby's breath, caraway, carrots (let them form flowers and seeds), cosmos, dill (let it go into flowering stage), feverfew, lavender, lemon balm, marigolds, nasturtiums, parsley, Queen Anne's Lace, rose-scented geraniums, sunflowers, sweet alyssum, thyme, white sage, and wildflowers local to your area. Some of these plants and herbs could become invasive so you might want to plant them around your garden's perimeter or in containers. A diverse selection of plants near the roses will bring in their defenders.

If they don't come fast enough or soon enough, you can also buy beneficial insects from local garden centers, Internet, or mail-order catalogues (see Sources).

The following insects can actually help your roses:

Aphid Midge—When I first noticed these mosquito-like flies with long legs and delicate, thin bodies, I eliminated them because I thought they would harm my plants or me. Then I learned that the tiny bright orange larvae feed on more than sixty species of aphids. Adults survive on pollen and nectar and will fly from flower to flower as they feed.

Ladybugs—You probably know that ladybugs or lady beetles are gardener's friends. Actually, it's their larvae that munch aphids, those annoying tiny critters that form columns on tender rose shoots and buds. As they suck sap from the plant, they weaken and disfigure them. Ladybug larvae suck out the life of an aphid and do a very good job of it. Each hungry baby can consume thirty or forty aphids daily. It helps if you know what they look like. They resemble tiny little alligators colored in black and red. If you see yellow-orange eggs under plant leaves, rejoice. These are ladybug eggs that will hatch if undisturbed.

Green or Brown Lacewings—The adults have gauzy wings attached to pale green bodies. Brown lacewings have brown wings and are smaller than their green relatives. As adults, they sip nectar from various plants. Their larvae, called aphid lions, are the insect eaters. They impale aphids and other soft-bodied insects and suck them dry.

Ground beetles—Although these large blue-black or dark brown beetles look fearsome, they don't harm plants. By day, they hide under rocks and boards. By night, they hunt snails, cutworms, gypsy moth larvae, and root maggots.

Praying mantids—Their fierce appearance is justified. These large mantids eat just about any type of insect, including honeybees. Their brown, twiggy appearance keeps them well camouflaged. You may be lucky enough to live in a region where they're living naturally. If not, you can buy egg cases at many nurseries.

Wasps—Although I fear their stings, I've learned to respect their value in rose gardens. Several varieties attack thrips and keep their population in check before they can disfigure white or pale roses.

Earthworms—It's hard to think of beneficial insects without including lowly earthworms, for without them, gardens would be barren. Aristotle referred to worms as "intestines of the earth." They can eat their own weight in decaying plant matter every day. Their tunneling activity and digestive byproducts (called "castings") help aerate soil and improve its structure and mineral content. You can buy various types of worms, but one of the surest ways of attracting them to your garden is by adding lots of organic matter to your soil.

These are the bugs that can really bug you and your roses:

Aphids—Colonies form on tender young canes, buds, and leaves, both under and on top. Every spring they appear, and disappear when temperatures climb over 90 or so degrees.

Ants protect and herd colonies of aphids like humans do to cattle. Ants feed on the sweet honeydew that aphids secrete. Black sooty mold can also appear on honeydew trails.

Thrips—These microscopic creatures enter buds of roses and suck the juices. You can tell their presence when buds turn brown, fail, or open incompletely. Thrips prefer white or pastel-colored flowers.

Japanese Beetles—Fortunately for people gardening west of the Rocky Mountains, these metallic blue or green beetles with coppery wings aren't a problem. It's another story elsewhere, where they can ravage roses and other plants. There are traps available or try handpicking and disposing.

Leafhoppers—Several different species of these slender one-eighth-inch-long bugs suck plant juices. As they hop from plant to plant, they can also spread viral diseases. Fortunately, lacewings consume their eggs.

Spider mites—Although technically not insects, they're considerable pests in rose gardens, especially in hot weather when they can rapidly defoliate roses as they suck juices from leaves, beginning at the bottom. Ladybugs and lacewings feast on them and they can also be controlled by blasts of water.

You can attract beneficial insects at the same time you camouflage bare rose canes with companion plants. Try sweet alyssum, dwarf yarrow, or marigolds.

Outwit Summer Pests

IN SUMMER, ROSE GARDEN STRATEGY shifts from flower production to plant protection. Close observation of plants and a little tender loving care will help your roses survive hungry insects that attack in summer. Different pests predominate at different times in the growing season. Right now, spider mites top the list of potential problems. You can tell if your roses are under attack by spider mites when the leaves drop off the plant, beginning at the bottom and quickly progressing to the top. Leaves that are on the plant can look distorted and may be spotted with yellow, red, or brown. This happens because these microscopic mites suck sap from leaves. In a severe infestation, you can see webs underneath the leaves.

Fortunately, spider mites easily succumb to blasts of water directed from a hose up through the plants. Thoroughly wet the undersides of leaves where they congregate. Spider mites reproduce very quickly, so be sure to repeat for at least three days in a row. Once the mites are gone, the rose bush will recover and produce new leaves. If you think you aren't solving the mite problem, you can use a non-toxic approach such as spraying the leaves, both top and bottom, with a solution of insecticidal soap mixed according to the directions on the package.

High temperatures usually kill off pests like aphids, which flourish in spring. But if you still find some colonies forming along the stems and buds, you can control them with blasts of water from a hose. Or, you can let Mother Nature handle them. They're a favorite food of ladybugs and lacewings.

Summer is also a time when you might notice a number of green spiders hanging around your roses. These are welcome visitors because they eat insect pests. They're another reason to avoid toxic chemicals.

Also, you might notice wasps hovering above your rose buds. Resist the temptation to run for the bug spray. I've observed them from a respectful distance and checked with a local entomologist who confirmed my observations. Wasps are meat eaters, and they, too, are feasting on the bad bugs among your roses. They target thrips, tiny insects that burrow into petals and suck sap. Thrips have invaded if flower petal edges turn brown. They enter while the bud is so tight that sprays can't penetrate, so predators are the most effective control. If you must take some action, try insecticidal soap or rotenone, mixed according to package directions.

Grasshoppers are a problem in my garden. I've watched adults chew leaves and flower petals. I've become so annoyed at their interference with my roses that I've even resorted to grabbing them with my hand shears and instantly dispatching them. Long-handled pruning shears are excellent for this purpose; the grasshoppers don't anticipate their demise.

Garlic is said to banish evil spirits and can also keep insects away. Try one of the new garlic-based insecticides now available in nurseries. Some plants have properties that repel garden pests. Try planting catnip, marigold, radish, or garlic around your rose bushes.

I also keep bird feeders well-filled to encourage their presence in my garden. Birds are very effective insect controllers, and many times I've watched in delight as mockingbirds harvest grasshoppers to feed their hungry brood. This is the ultimate joy in outwitting bad bugs.

Colonies of aphids can be destroyed by hosing them off the tender new rose growth they prefer. Be sure to wash under the leaves and repeat for at least four days since new aphids hatch daily.

Poor Wet Roses
fighting fungal diseases

APRIL SHOWERS BRING MAY FLOWERS, forecasts the popular rhyme. But when nature brings May deluges those May flowers can show adverse effects from lashing torrents of rain. This happened in my garden one year during a season of especially heavy storms. Some rose blossoms were knocked off their stems. Other bushes had canes bending towards the ground, their opened blooms weighted down by water accumulating in their petals. Many blossoms failed to open at all, but instead "balled" and turned pasty brown as petals rotted from fungal disease.

If you live in a region where there's a lot of rain, your roses will likely be attacked by annoying fungal diseases—powdery mildew, downy mildew, and rust. Blackspot is another fungus commonly seen in wet climates like that of the Pacific Northwest or England. Even roses that are normally very disease-resistant can be affected during periods of extreme rain. One of my all-time favorite roses is 'Sally Holmes' because it's vigorous, very free-flowering, and usually very healthy. However, during an El Niño episode, I noticed powdery mildew on some leaves.

If you're wondering what has gotten on your roses, you can identify the culprits by looking closely at the tops and undersides of leaves. Powdery mildew shows up as a fine white film that covers leaves and even rose stems, especially just under the buds. Downy mildew is a fairly new disease. High humidity, cool temperatures, and lots of fog and drizzle are necessary for this fungus to thrive. Affected rose leaves have purplish-red to dark brown spots. Diseased leaves can fall off the plants.

Rust is easy to spot. Check under the rose leaves for yellow pustules. This troublesome

disease can also cause leaves to turn brown, wither, and drop as the fungal disease progresses.

If your rose leaves have black circles with irregular margins, you're observing blackspot. As these fungal colonies grow, they can become surrounded by yellow. This disease will cause leaves to drop off and can distort flowers.

There are several things a conscientious gardener can do to combat rust, mildew, and blackspot. For starters, it's also important to be sure your roses have good air circulation by not crowding them. If you have the time and energy, the best action is to remove all diseased leaves and discard them (don't add them to your compost pile). Clean up all fallen leaves as well. Then spray all bushes, being sure to get the spray solution on the top and undersides of the leaves. Just a few years ago, rose experts recommended use of chemical fungicides to control diseases. But because of increasing awareness of the harmful effects these toxic chemicals have on soil, water, birds, and beneficial insects, there's more interest and information now about using nontoxic methods for controlling rose diseases. There are several commercial products of benign fungicides, including a sulfur-based one from Safer, Inc., and Rose Defense, which contains neem oil. You can also make your own.

Sharon Van Enoo, a Consulting Rosarian and rose exhibitor uses baking soda and vinegar with excellent results. She recommends spraying at least two weeks consecutively for best results.

If you don't mind the damage, or object to the time spent spraying, you can also patiently wait for the weather to change. Once temperatures climb and rains disappear, so do these fungal diseases.

To combat rust, midew, and blackspot, Sharon Van Enoo recommends using:

1 tablespoon baking soda
1 tablespoon vinegar
1 tablespoon canola oil

Combine ingredients in one gallon of warm water and stir thoroughly. Use a trigger-spray bottle to apply if you have just a few roses. A tank sprayer is useful if you have a large number of bushes. Be sure to wet the tops and bottoms of leaves. Repeat in approximately seven days with fresh solution.

Wasco Festival of Roses

T HE ROSE IS AMERICA'S MOST POPULAR FLOWER, its national flower, and its most popular garden plant. In Wasco, fifteen miles north of Bakersfield, California, the rose rules the economy and has put the small town on the map because of its fortunate combination of sandy soil, ample water, abundant sunshine, and mild winters.

More than sixty-five percent of all roses grown in the United States grow in the fields of Wasco (see photo, page 115). There, eleven major companies grow some forty-five million rose plants. In early September, five thousand acres of rose fields are in full, dazzling color, and the city celebrates by throwing a festival.

Approximately ten thousand rose enthusiasts and lovers of parties attend the event, which was inaugurated in 1969 by the Wasco Chamber of Commerce. The annual Wasco Festival of Roses celebrates the Queen of Flowers with a Wasco Rose Queen Pageant, parade, rose show, carnival, art show, pancake breakfast, barbecue lunch, golf tournament,

and five- and ten-kilometer run and walkathon. Every festival includes a featured rose and theme—for example, 'Peace' was featured during the "Country Rose" festival.

The festival highlight is a tour of the rose fields. Narrated, one-hour bus tours enable visitors to see all five thousand acres of those rose fields close-up. Each row contains approximately 2,500 rose plants. The wave of color upon color is breathtaking and can make even a non-gardener gasp. In addition to exclamations of awe and delight, sounds of clicking photo shutters permeate the tours. If you can only take a day trip, choose Saturday or Sunday, when the tour buses are in operation.

Festival events include a Rose Queen Pageant, tennis tournament, and carnival. An AARS-sanctioned rose show opens to the public on Saturday at noon, and continues on Sunday from 10 a.m. to 4 p.m. in Veteran's Memorial Hall. Dedicated rose hobbyists vie for trophies and ribbons, and the public can see meticulously groomed and displayed hybrid teas, floribundas, grandifloras, miniatures, shrubs, and Old Garden Roses.

The rose parade that begins at 10 a.m. on Saturday is more laid-back than Pasadena's famous extravaganza, but still offers lots of color, and numerous entries feature roses from local rose growers.

Naturally, an event devoted to roses also includes the opportunity to buy them. A wide variety of rose plants and types will be for sale at ten dollars per plant, thanks to the rose growers who donate them to the festival.

If you plan to spend a night or two, call ahead for motel reservations. There are two motels in Wasco—Cinderella (805-758-3068) and Wasco Inn Motel (805-758-5317). Lost Hills, located eighteen miles west of Wasco, offers a Motel Six (805-797-2524) and an Economy Inn (805-797-2371).

For information about the festival, contact the Wasco Festival of Roses office, 805-758-3068.

Public Rose Gardens

O NE OF THE BEST WAYS TO SELECT ROSES for your own garden is by seeing them in someone else's. Public rose gardens give you the opportunity to see a large selection, usually tagged so you know what you're viewing. An added bonus is that most public gardens contain mature plants so you'll know the size and shape a certain variety assumes as it ages. Also, flower colors are deceptive in catalogues. See a rose in a climate similar to yours and you'll be certain of its appearance in your own garden. The following are among America's best.

The Huntington Rose Garden, San Marino, California

Among the pleasures of living in California is the ability to garden or enjoy other people's gardens during winter. While much of the nation shivers and shovels snow, we can experience greenery and flowers.

One very pleasant place to experience gardens is at the Huntington in San Marino. This great estate, once the property of Henry E. and Arabella Huntington, includes a world-famous library, art gallery, and botanic garden. In addition to a passion for collecting art and books, the Huntingtons also collected plants. These plants formed the basis of the extensive botanical gardens, including a romantic and yet very practical rose garden.

The three-acre rose garden was designed in 1908 by Los Angeles architects Myron Hunt and Elmer Grey as a strolling and cutting garden. Ranch superintendent William Hertich planted out fifty to one hundred each of more than two hundred different varieties of roses. Spring bulbs were interplanted for a massive display of spring color.

Today, the public is invited to stroll beneath rose-laden pergolas and admire the approximately four thousand roses, consisting of 1,500 cultivars that make up the collection.

Although the roses are pruned back each winter in preparation for mid-April bloom, the rose garden is always worth visiting.

"We redesigned the rose garden in the 1980s to make it more inviting to people and also to establish it as a resource for gardeners who want to observe how well specific roses grow in Southern California," explained Clair Martin, curator of the rose garden.

All roses are labeled so enthusiasts can note which varieties capture their fancy. And there's quite a choice, ranging from prehistoric species roses through two thousand years of rose history.

This is a formal rose garden, so termed because it is arranged in beds. There are forty such beds at the Huntington, organized by years in which specific varieties were grown or hybridized. Old Garden Roses, those grown before 1867, occupy one long bed along the north pergola. You can see 'Autumn Damask', a rose enjoyed by Greeks and Romans, or 'Safrano' or 'Old Blush', early tea roses imported from China.

Early hybrid tea roses, including the first, 'La France', introduced in 1867, occupy another bed. Stroll past roses from the 1920s, like 'Talisman', or the 1930s, containing an old favorite, 'Herbert Hoover', or the 1940s, where you can view 'Charlotte Armstrong'. The adjacent herb garden contains redolent Old Garden Roses, including examples of Rugosa, Noisette, and Hybrid Musks, used for cosmetic and medicinal purposes centuries ago.

Continue the stroll past modern roses and winners of the coveted All-America Rose Selections (AARS) awards.

Benches are placed strategically throughout the garden, clustered under magnificent magnolia trees and along the sweeping St. Augustine Lawn. Visitors are encouraged to walk along the lawn and view the beds of English and French shrub roses planted in the garden's interior. Martin was one of the first to appreciate the English roses developed by David Austin, and the Huntington grows 115 of the 120 Austin varieties available in the United States.

The Huntingtons used to stroll along a central walkway, beneath stately arches now covered with a collection of climbing roses, including the antique 'Belle of Portugal' and the new, multihued 'Polka'. Visitors can continue in their footsteps to a massive twenty-foot dome, covered with myriad blossoms of 'Mermaid'.

In addition to being a research garden, this rose garden evokes romance. A winding pathway leads to an eighteenth-century French stone tempietto (little temple) containing a statue entitled Love, the Captive of Youth, depicting Cupid and his captor, a fair maiden. A bed of 'French Lace' roses encircles the setting.

A pleasant way to end the visit is to experience afternoon tea in the adjacent tea room, where a buffet of tea sandwiches, pastries, cheese, crackers, and assorted beverages is served. This is a popular destination and reservations are advised.

The Huntington is open Tuesday through Friday, noon to 4:30 p.m.; Saturday and Sunday, 10:30 a.m. to 4:30 p.m. For information about admission, call 626-405-2100.

The Wrigley Gardens, Pasadena, California

Visit the Wrigley Gardens at Tournament House in January to view two thousand rose bushes in impressive bloom. At this time of year, rose bushes in much of the nation are already bedded down in protective coverings of straw, mulch, or burlap for a long winter slumber. Even in this benign climate, many rose gardeners encourage their rose bushes to slow down for the season by withholding fertilizer and encouraging rose hips to form, signaling the bush to stop flowering.

But the roses in the Wrigley Garden are blooming as though it were still spring, thanks to the efforts of volunteers from the Pacific Rose Society who have been nurturing and caring for the prized plants year-round since 1989.

The gardens attract attention year-round, but special notice comes in conjunction with the annual Rose Parade on January 1, when the cameras of the world are focused on the former Wrigley mansion.

"We try to have the roses in full bloom at this time of year and the garden looks as though it's spring," explained garden director Bartje Miller. Miller, an Altadena resident and a member of the Pacific Rose Society for almost fifty years, spearheaded the effort for the society to assume custodianship of the famed rose garden. She contacted officials at the Tournament of Roses in 1989 and persuaded Chris Greenwood, the society's president at that time, to support the plan. A loyal and hardworking group of society members enthusiastically agreed to renovate and rejuvenate the existing rose garden and provide weekly maintenance. Most of the bushes were removed, the soil rejuvenated, and new roses obtained from the major growers—Armstrong (now part of Jackson & Perkins), J & P, and Weeks Roses. Greenwood dug more planting holes than he cares to remember, and each rose was carefully planted under Miller's supervision and according to her design.

Every Tuesday morning, armed with pruning shears, keen knowledge, and love of roses, the stalwart group removes the spent blooms and makes sure the rose garden is in tip-top condition. (A professional gardening firm weeds and maintains the automatic sprinklers.) Once a month, they sprinkle granular fertilizer around each bush. Volunteers include Kenneth Miller, Bartje's husband who is a skilled rosarian and former estate gardener, Bill and Wanda Knights, Norman Nelson, Bob Rowe, and Angie Bobbett, an eighty-two-year-old Pasadena resident who rarely misses a week in the Wrigley Rose Garden.

"I'm actually in the garden at least three times a week," Miller explained. "I like to keep my eyes on any newly planted bushes or just check that everything's O.K. That garden's really a part of me."

Their efforts have been acknowledged by Tournament officials who installed a granite plaque in 1991 honoring the Pacific Rose Society. The plaque states the garden is "dedicated to all who enjoy roses."

In 1994, the AARS gave its Public Rose Garden Award to the Tournament of Roses Association. A plaque installed in the North Garden commemorates the award and states, "For contributing to the public interest in rose growing through its efforts in maintaining an outstanding public rose garden."

The Wrigley Garden is open, free of charge, year-round except December 31 through January 2, when the Rose Parade takes center stage. Then, when the excitement ends, the viewing stands are removed, and the cameras are focused elsewhere, the Pacific Rose Society members give the roses their annual winter pruning.

But before that happens, grab a friend or visiting relation and enjoy America's national flower. Each variety is clearly identified. This is an excellent way to see varieties that you might think of adding to your own garden. Or even if you don't have a green thumb, you can stroll the paths, pause by the fountain, sniff a fragrant blossom, and enjoy the beauty and majesty of the queen of flowers.

The Wrigley Gardens, Tournament House, 391 S. Orange Grove Boulevard, Pasadena, California.

Rose Hills Memorial Park, Whittier, California

I fell in love with roses in 1983 and planted a dozen bushes in the front yard of my Los Angeles home. When they failed to thrive, I realized I needed help. It came from an unlikely place—a cemetery. Rose Hills Memorial Park, in Whittier, contains one of Southern California's great rose gardens. At the time I first saw it, it was under the direction of Jim Kirk. He held pruning demonstrations and freely offered advice to rose enthusiasts about how to grow the queen of flowers. Like hundreds of other fellow rose enthusiasts, we were educated and entertained at these pruning events.

I didn't return to Rose Hills until recently, at the urging of Tom Carruth. He told me the garden had been renovated and expanded. In his opinion, it's now one of the best rose gardens in America, yet its reputation hasn't kept up with its beauty.

When I viewed the ten-acre garden, overflowing with close to ten thousand gorgeous rose bushes in full bloom, I understood why Tom praised it so highly. Unlike most rose gardens, where individual varieties are planted in regimented rows, the Pageant of Roses Garden at Rose Hills is about mass display. Here are eighty-four different planting beds, in various sizes and shapes, with most containing fifty plants of the same variety. This mass display creates stunning vistas of rich color and, in many cases, luscious fragrance.

The garden contains proven performers like 'Double Delight', 'Angel Face', 'The Fairy', 'Mr. Lincoln', 'Peace', 'Redgold', and 'Ingrid Bergman' (the world's favorite rose). There are also new varieties like 'Veteran's Honor', 'Diana, Princess of Wales', 'Betty Boop', 'Starry Night', and 'Cherry Parfait'. This is a pleasant garden for strolling, enjoying fragrance and flower form, or sitting on one of the benches under a shade tree. It's a place for beauty, contemplation, and reflection, appropriate to the setting at one of the region's major cemeteries.

In 1914, August H. Gregg, a member of one of Whittier's pioneer families, established Whittier Heights Memorial Park as a serene place of peace and beauty to serve the burial needs of a burgeoning community. Whittier was founded in 1887 as a Quaker colony on what was once part of the Rancho Paso de Bartolo Spanish land grant, at one time owned by Pio Pico, the last governor of Mexican California. His cattle-grazing fields were transformed into citrus orchards by subsequent owners, before the establishment of the memorial park.

Parts of the grounds include the Puente hillsides, studded with wild mustard, oak trees, and grasslands. Frank B. Gibson, a prominent Los Angeles landscape architect in the early twentieth century, created the first layout. Over the next few decades, owners bought more land, expanded the cemetery, changed the name to Rose Hills Memorial Park and used roses to decorate perimeter fences and to serve as the official emblem. By 1959, it consisted of 2,600 acres—four times the size of the National Cemetery at Arlington, Virginia.

This was a milestone year for rose enthusiasts, when the initial rose garden was created with the assistance of the late John H. van Barnveld, a local director of the American Rose Society. Together with John D. Gregg, then president of Rose Hills, a rose garden foundation was formed and the formal rose garden created. A local landscape architectural firm, Cornell, Bridgers and Troller, designed what at that time was a three-acre garden and Barnveld selected the varieties for display. The garden was an immediate success with the public when it opened in April 1959.

As time progressed, the garden grew in size and plantings. When Jim Kirk assumed the position of curator in the 1970s, he began the popular January pruning demonstrations and other events. By 1984, the garden was so well regarded that the AARS Public Gardens Committee awarded its Outstanding Public Garden Achievement Award to this garden.

However, time started to take its toll and many of the bushes became old and exhausted by the 1990s. In 1999, a major renovation took place, this time under the guidance of rosarian Dr. Tommy Cairns, president of the American Rose Society, and garden supervisor Fred Patritti. The result is a meticulously planted and maintained rose garden that is California's largest public display of modern roses.

Dr. Cairns selected most of the roses for this garden, using specific criteria. His aim is to show the rose-loving public that roses are excellent landscape plants suitable for most garden settings. Visitors can see a wide diversity of colors, shapes, forms, and sizes, from tiny groundcovers to tall climbers, some trained as "weeping trees" cascading in umbrella shapes.

In addition to the weeping trees, Dr. Cairns created a sophisticated garden containing five thousand red and white roses near the administration building. Its center is a fifty-foot circular bed planted with standard tree roses including red 'Europeana' and white 'Honor' and 'Iceberg'. Additional beds surround it and contain more roses in the form of standards or bushes, rimmed with miniature varieties like red 'Santa Claus', white 'Gourmet Popcorn', and white 'Pillow Fight'.

"The French tradition of remembrance is with red and white poppies," explained Dr. Cairns. "We're using roses instead."

He has also included roses like Tom's floribunda 'Hot Cocoa' with novel colors. Fragrance is important, too, and a number of varieties, including David Austin English Roses, beckon visitors with their strong aromas. Dr. Cairn's favorite in this old-fashioned-looking group is pink 'Mary Rose'. Some of the beds contain both large and small rose bushes to illustrate how to combine groups of roses for striking color effects—like mauve 'Angel Face' edged with yellow miniature 'Sun Sprinkles'.

Several test gardens are also on display for the public, including an AARS test garden, one of just twenty-two in the U.S. You can view the future winners and would-be winners of the AARS award, although they're identified only by number during the two-year evaluation process. An international rose trial garden and a miniature rose trial garden are also on view.

The Pageant of Roses garden at Rose Hills Memorial Park is located at 3888 S. Workman Mill Road, Whittier. It's open daily from 8:00 a.m. to 8:00 p.m., free of charge. For information, call 562-699-0921 or visit the Web site at www.rosehills.com.

The Nixon Library, Whittier, California

Whittier is famous also as the region where Richard Nixon spent his childhood (he was born in nearby Yorba Linda). The simple house where he was born in 1910 has been preserved and is part of the Nixon Library, site of his grave (alongside Pat Nixon). The library also contains three acres of gardens where mass plantings of roses are combined with perennials, annuals, and other colorful plants, selected for their association with the thirty-seventh president of the United States and his first lady. The display begins in the parking lot, where one hundred white 'Honor' rose bushes showcase rows of the vivid red 'Veteran's Honor'. Another corner contains fifty 'Sunset Celebration' bushes and nearby are fifty regal 'Gold Medal' bushes.

The gardens at the Nixon Library consist of several distinct themes: a California formal garden, the Pat Nixon Amphitheater, the Birthplace garden, the First Lady's Garden, and the Memorial Garden. The California garden surrounds a 210-foot-long reflecting pool. Slender Queen palm trees flank the pool and their reflection is vivid on a bright California day. This is a formal garden, with long walks, boxwood parterres containing 'Iceberg' roses, crepe myrtle trees, heliotrope, and bay laurel trees. Large terra-cotta planters filled with vivid red azaleas line the walkways.

This garden leads to the Pat Nixon Amphitheater, a large grassy site used for receptions and special events. More than 150 'Mr. Lincoln' roses line one side. Here, too, are 'Pat Nixon' roses—a red floribunda named in her honor—fifteen different kinds of lavender, a large planting of 'Madame Alfred Carriere' shaped as trees and underplanted with soft pink 'Dove'. Nearby is a bed with several varieties of David Austin English roses: 'Tamora', 'Abraham Darby', and 'Cressida'. The color is echoed in an adjacent bed containing richly fragrant 'Just Joey'. Another perimeter is lined with 120 'Peace' roses.

The Nixon birthplace is beyond and a cottage garden surrounds the simple house, which is open for public tour. Built in 1912 by Frank and Hannah Nixon, the small farmhouse is surrounded with plants evoking that era—hollyhocks, Henrii lilies, calla lilies, salvia, and single roses like 'Dainty Bess', 'White Wings', and 'Angel Wings'.

Leaving the house, visitors pass the Frank Nixon pepper tree, planted in 1912. Further along the path is the Memorial Garden, surrounding the two graves. Here are two hundred 'Double Delight' roses, along with more roses and many perennial plants favored by the former first lady, who loved gardens.

Nearby is the First Lady's Garden, containing all roses named in honor of first ladies: 'Lady Bird Johnson', 'Betty Ford', 'Roselyn Carter', 'First Lady Nancy' (Reagan), 'Barbara Bush', and more 'Pat Nixon'. According to rose curator Kevin Cartwright, the 'Pat Nixon' rose is almost always in bloom, even in winter. It's appropriate to the stated purpose of this garden. "It reflects Pat Nixon's love of gardens and of people," Cartwright said while escorting me through the gardens. "She was an amateur horticulturist who at the San Clemente Western White House gardened with her own hands. At the White House, she opened the gardens periodically so the public could enjoy their beauty."

Visiting this garden is a memorable way to experience a legacy of beauty and serenity.

The Nixon Library is located at 18001 Yorba Linda Boulevard, Yorba Linda. Open daily (except Thanksgiving and Christmas) from 10 a.m. to 5 p.m., Sundays 11 am to 5 p.m.

Admission ranges from $2 to $5.95. For information call 714-993-5075 or visit www.nixonlibrary.org.

World Peace Rose Garden, Sacramento, California

Dedicated in 2003, the World Peace Rose Garden displays 650 roses representing 145 different varieties in a formal Victorian design on a one-half acre site. Planned and developed by J. L. David and Sylvia Villalobes, this garden showcases modern roses "that knock your socks off and really awe you," according to David. The garden is dedicated to the concept of world peace, and many of the roses symbolize this, such as the beloved hybrid tea 'Peace', which represented hope for a better world after World War II. Its offspring, 'Lasting Peace', 'Desert Peace', 'Chicago Peace', and also 'Love and Peace' are included here. There is a series of roses named to honor war veterans: 'Bronze Star', 'Silver Star', and 'World War II Memorial'. In addition, visitors can enjoy exceptionally fragrant varieties like 'Double Delight', 'Lemon Spice', 'Mr. Lincoln', and 'Eiffel Tower'. Walkways lead to a small courtyard with a fountain in the center. A heart-shaped seating wall surrounds an elegant Peace Pavilion, an open-air gazebo where public and civic events take place. Numerous benches are placed throughout this garden so visitors can sit, contemplate, and enjoy its serenity. Additional inspiration comes from the many plaques inscribed with messages of peace that were written by American children and submitted as part of the dedication ceremonies.

The World Peace Memorial Garden is located in California State Capitol Park at 15th near L Street, Sacramento, California. It's open daily from dawn to dusk. For information, call 800-205-1223.

The International Rose Test Garden, Portland, Oregon

Three renowned rose gardens in Portland beckon rose lovers who come from all over to enjoy one of the world's most famous rose gardens, the International Rose Test Garden. Containing more than eight thousand rose bushes, it began in 1917 when three nurserymen decided that Portland was an ideal location in which to test and trial roses from around the world. At that time, Portland was already regarded as the "City of Roses" because of its two hundred miles of rose-bordered streets. With the assistance of members of the American Rose Society, the garden was designed and planted in time to serve as a safe haven for hybrid roses grown in Europe during World War I. Fearing these unique plants might be destroyed in the war, rose growers from many European nations sent their plants to Portland and the garden's success was immediately ensured.

The International Rose Test Garden is located in Washington Park, at 400 SW Kingston, Portland, Oregon, and is open daily from 7:30 a.m. to 9:00 p.m.

Peninsula Park Rose Garden, Portland, Oregon

Further north is Peninsula Park Rose Garden, a formal garden containing more than 8,900 rose bushes displayed on two acres within a sixteen-acre park. The city purchased the park in 1909 for $60,000. Originally owned by local businesswoman Liverpool Liz, it had been the site for a roadhouse and racetrack for quarter-mile horse racing. Oregon architects Ellis Lawrence and Ormond R. Bean designed the park, which was completed in 1913.

Many of the original features remain, including the lantern-style streetlights, stone pillars, vast brickwork, and the hundred-year-old fountain found in the center of the rose garden. This was Portland's first public rose garden and many antique roses are included in this formal landscape. Visitors are greeted by stunning displays of sixty-five rose varieties that border the steps leading to the sunken rose garden. When first created, it was the showplace of its time, attracting 300,000 visitors during its first year. Even now, the mature and graceful plants attract many admirers who wander the grass paths and view the dowagers encased in precisely hedged display beds.

Located at 700 N. Portland Boulevard, Portland, this garden is open daily.

Ladd's Addition, Portland, Oregon

The smallest and most intimate of the three Portland rose gardens, Ladd's Addition is located in a historic residential area just across the river from downtown. The property had been part of a farm owned by William Sargeant Ladd, a wealthy businessman during the mid-nineteenth century when he also served as mayor of Portland. In 1909 Portland's first park director, Emanuel Mische, designed a formal landscape plan for the gardens in Ladd's Addition. He planted camellias, perennials, and a large lawn in a central circle. Numerous rose varieties were planted in four diamonds, evoking a stained glass effect on one and a half acres. Additional roses are planted in precise designs in the three blocks surrounding this garden.

Located at SE Ladd & Harrison Streets, Portland, open daily. For further information about the gardens of Portland, call 503-823-3636 or visit www.portlandparks.org.

Richmond Rose Garden, Richmond, Indiana

Richmond calls itself "Rose City" because it's the home of Hills Rose Growers, premier rose growers and marketers of cut roses for the floral trade. City officials decided to create a public rose garden to honor the city's rose heritage and established this All-America Rose Garden in 1987. Combining European and Victorian design, it contains two thousand rose varieties with annuals, perennials, and ornamental trees as companion plantings. Within the overall landscape are several distinct gardens, including one of 139 AARS public display rose gardens in America, which contains the AARS winning roses for the past sixty years. Modern German roses are featured in the Richmond Friendship Garden Peak, which celebrates an association with Zweibruken, Germany.

A Victorian gazebo is available for weddings and special events. This garden is especially attractive during peak bloom times in June and September.

Located in Glen Miller Park, 2500 National Road East, Richmond, Indiana. For details, call 765-962-1638.

Cranford Rose Garden, Brooklyn Botanic Garden, New York

The Cranford Rose Garden, which opened in 1928 at the Brooklyn Botanic Garden, is widely regarded as one of the largest and finest in America. It's an excellent garden in which to study the historic development of roses, from Old Garden Roses to current hybrid teas. Roses of various shapes and forms are on display. Upright hybrid teas, polyanthas, and floribundas are massed in rectangular central beds, approached by grassy swaths of pathways. Other types of roses that ramble, climb, trail, or spread are planted on the perimeter on an assortment of structures. Climbing roses clamber up concrete posts, swing up over metal arches spanning the walkway surrounding the center section, or sprawl over chains. In border beds, old garden roses climb up cedar posts. In between are species roses, and in the background, modern climbers and ramblers are trained on latticework enclosing the garden.

The garden is named for Walter V. Cranford, a construction engineer whose firm built many of Brooklyn's subway tunnels. When he read a report that a rose garden was planned, he donated the $10,000 needed to make it a reality. Excavation began in June 1927 and construction was completed in November. Initially, one thousand rose bushes were planted in the one-acre garden. In 1928, an additional two thousand were installed, representing 650 different species and varieties. Many of these plants still remain in the garden. Over the years, additional varieties planted include miniatures and modern types so there are now 5,000 plants of 1,000 different varieties on display.

Education is an important aspect of this garden, and each variety is labeled by name and date of introduction. This is an excellent place to view historic roses and mature plants, and also see varieties that thrive in an urban location that has hot and humid summers and harsh winters.

Brooklyn Botanic Garden is located at 1000 Washington Avenue, Brooklyn, New York.

Open April–September, Tuesday through Friday, from 8:00 a.m. to 6 p.m., Saturday, Sunday, 10:00 a.m. to 6 p.m. From October through March, the closing hour is 4:30 p.m.

Admission is charged except Saturdays from 10 a.m. to noon. For information, call 718-623-7200.

Elizabeth Park, West Hartford, Connecticut

The area now known as Elizabeth Park was the private estate of Charles Pond, a wealthy industrialist and businessman. At his death, he willed it to the City of Hartford, with the condition that it be used as a horticultural park named in honor of his wife, who had predeceased him. Frederick Law Olmsted and Son designed Elizabeth Park to include expanses of meadows, fields, and water. Within the 102-acre park is a two-acre rose garden, containing fifteen thousand rose bushes of eight hundred varieties. Peak bloom is late June and July.

Elizabeth Park is located at Prospect & Asylum Avenues, West Hartford, Connecticut. For details, call 860-722-4321.

The American Rose Society, Shreveport, Louisiana

The headquarters of the American Rose Society, this 118-acre site contains one of the largest rose gardens in America (see photo, page 126). Consisting of sixty-five individual gardens, it showcases twenty-two thousand rose bushes representing four hundred varieties of antique and modern roses displayed in a variety of settings. Here visitors can view Old Garden Roses in the Hudson Heritage Collection, prize-winning show roses in the Horizon Roses Garden, and the Peterson Garden, consisting of ramblers, species, and hybrid musk roses blooming among hostas, woodland ferns, and other shade-loving plants.

Beds of AARS winners flank an imposing Windsounds Carillon Tower, the focal point of the landscape. Another attraction is a three-tiered fountain adjacent to the Thigpen-Harold Administration Building and gift shop. Also popular is a rustic chapel, site of numerous weddings each spring and summer when the roses are in full bloom.

Other theme parks are the tranquil Durham Japanese Tea Garden, featuring an authentic tea house, traditional tobi ishi stepping stone pathway, and a kasuga-style lantern.

The ARS garden is a popular attraction for rose lovers and for families. Children enjoy the butterfly garden, which displays plants that attract many of these colorful winged creatures. There's also a children's playground and adjoining picnic grove. Annual events include guided tours, symposiums, and rose festivals. Every winter, the garden is heavily decorated with twinkling lights.

The American Rose Center is located at 8877 Jefferson-Paige Road, Shreveport, Louisiana. Open daily. For details, call 318-938-5402.

Notable New Roses
AARS *winners and more*

E VERY YEAR ROSE LOVERS MUST DECIDE which of the dozens of new varieties deserve a place of honor in their gardens. All-America Rose Selections (AARS), a non-profit association for rose research and promotion, offers a solution. Since 1938, AARS has conducted a trial program in which roses are planted and identified only by a number, then evaluated carefully for two years at test gardens throughout the United States. AARS judges score rose plants for fifteen traits, including color, disease resistance, bud and flower form, vigor, hardiness, growth habit, foliage, and fragrance. Only the best of the best earn the designation of AARS winner.

1998

There were four AARS winners for 1998—two hybrid tea roses, one grandiflora, and one shrub rose.

'Sunset Celebration' has a lovely apricot color. It's a fascinating creamy apricot amber blend that evokes the hues of a lingering sunset. The rose is named in honor of *Sunset Magazine*'s one hundredth anniversary. An upright grower with large blooms, this winner has also earned the prestigious gold medal at the Hague. The flowers have a moderate fruity fragrance. It may take a year or two to get established, so give it time.

Red roses are perennial favorites, and the debut of the 1998 AARS winner 'Opening Night', hybridized by Keith Zary, vice president of research for Jackson & Perkins, won rave reviews immediately because of its true, bright red, long-lasting flowers on generous cutting stems.

Shrub roses continue to be popular, and the crop of 1998 AARS winners include 'First Light', a compact, rounded bush that tucks well into most landscapes. Each plant covers itself with masses of single-petaled flowers with burgundy stamens. The somewhat spicy fragrance is an extra bonus.

Adventurous gardeners with a love of bright colors can consider AARS winner 'Fame!', a grandiflora with large hot pink flowers, also the work of Zary for J&P. 'Fame!' dazzles the eyes, but not the nose, as it has little fragrance.

If you want fragrance in a rose, consider 'Sheila's Perfume', a gorgeous floribunda resembling a small hybrid tea. Bred by an amateur English hybridizer who named the delightful rose for his wife, 'Sheila's Perfume' is redolent with a strong fruit and rose perfume. The high-centered flowers are yellow brushed by deep pink, and the plant is an upright grower with glossy deep green leaves.

Nostalgia fans may be lured by two new floribunda roses named 'George Burns' and 'Gracie Allen'. The late, much-loved comedian personally selected the rose in honor of his wife, reports Tom Carruth, director of research for Weeks Roses in Upland, and hybridizer of these roses. He said Burns chose the plant because it produces white flowers with a pink heart and "it made him laugh and feel good." His namesake rose is as bright and cheery as the late comedian with yellow, red, pink, and cream striped petals with strong, sweet fragrance.

Usually, roses that don't win AARS awards are destroyed, never to grace our gardens. But in 1998, J&P made an exception and marketed two varieties that were among the top ten contenders for AARS designation, according to Zary, whose breeding program includes modern versions of old-fashioned roses. 'Rose Sachet' and 'Fragrant Lace' are the current results of that effort, and he promises more to come in the near future.

'Rose Sachet' is a hybrid tea with an unusual dusky pink color. The large, very fragrant flowers are quartered when fully opened. This rose is noteworthy because it combines fragrance with very good disease resistance, a breakthrough in rose breeding that hybridizers have only recently accomplished. 'Fragrant Lace' is also a brand new rose that could be at home in Queen Victoria's time with its ruffled light pink flowers and a yellow reverse, edged in darker pink. Also very disease-resistant, 'Fragrant Lace' has a fruity, citrus fragrance.

Fans of climbing roses can cheer because 1998 brought several outstanding new varieties including 'Cl. Berries 'n Cream' and 'Cl. Shadow Dancer.' 'Cl. Berries 'n Cream' is a very free-flowering, vigorous climber bearing masses of striped flowers with old rose pink and creamy white. Because it blooms on new and old wood, unlike many climbers that only bloom on old growth, the climber bears flowers even in the first year of planting. I've had one for two years, and am delighted with the strong, long stems (perfect for cutting), strong repeat, and mild apple fragrance.

Another workhorse of a climber is 'Cl. Shadow Dancer', the work of legendary hybridizer Ralph Moore who has won much acclaim with his miniature roses. 'Shadow Dancer' is a modest grower, eight feet in much of the nation, larger in milder climates. Blooming on new and old wood, the plant produces ruffled clusters of large flowers swirled with two tones of pink. The glossy green foliage is very disease-resistant.

2000

For 2000, three AARS winners were added to this distinctive collection—'Knock Out', 'Crimson Bouquet', and 'Gemini'.

'Knock Out' is a nicely rounded shrub rose that produces clusters of bright cherry red flowers, with single flower form, for most of the year. The shiny blue-green foliage is very disease-resistant. This is a lovely landscape rose, but don't expect much fragrance. This is a breakthrough shrub because it is immune to blackspot, a nasty disease in much of the U.S.

Excellent red roses are hard to breed, and the new 2000 winner, 'Crimson Bouquet', is a welcome addition for anyone who loves red roses. This variety is a grandiflora that is shorter and more rounded than usual for this category. The bold, brilliant red flowers are produced in clusters, in typical grandiflora style, and the plant's foliage is deep glossy green with strong disease resistance. Alas, the flower lures with color, but not fragrance.

The third winner is a hybrid tea rose, 'Gemini'. This rose is an upright and vigorous grower, and produces large double coral pink and rich cream blossoms. The blooms slowly spiral open to reveal four-inch flowers with twenty-five to thirty petals. This classic rose, which features long cutting stems, is highly resistant to disease. Again, fragrance is slight.

If you want to include a new rose with a lovely perfume, consider 'Barbra Streisand', the new creation of Tom Carruth. Personally selected by the legendary entertainer, Streisand's namesake rose is equally alluring with a powerful perfume and a striking mauve color. The glossy deep green foliage is disease-resistant.

Another noteworthy rose from Carruth is a yellow floribunda that is sold exclusively through Armstrong Gardens Centers. This firm selected and named the vibrant yellow rose 'John-John'.

"This rose is a tribute to the memory of a small boy who played at his father's feet while John F. Kennedy conducted the affairs of state," explained Chris Greenwood, director of public relations for Armstrong Garden Centers, Monrovia. "Free-flowering with sprays of yellow, this rose will provide the homeowner with months of carefree color."

Carruth bred the rose in 1992, and it has been growing in trial gardens throughout the U.S. 'John-John' is being sold solely in Southern California because in this region it has excellent disease resistance; however, it is prone to blackspot in other parts of the nation.

2001

In 2001, the AARS winners were 'Glowing Peace', a grandiflora; 'Sun Sprinkles', a miniature; and 'Marmalade Skies', a floribunda. This was one of the few years when a hybrid tea variety wasn't among the winners. Perhaps this is an indication of the changing taste of American gardeners. Where once the standard of beauty was the high-centered elegant bud-and-flower form of a tea rose, now the attractive appearance of the entire rose bush is also highly regarded by garden enthusiasts who value their use in landscapes.

'Glowing Peace' was created by the famed French House of Meilland, the same company that created the beloved 'Peace' rose. 'Glowing Peach' was named for its illustrious grandparent. Although 'Peace' is a hybrid tea, its offspring is a round, bushy grandiflora that grows to four feet by three feet. Its large, round buds open to three-inch blossoms of golden yellow and cantaloupe-orange blended petals, with light tea fragrance. This variety is very disease-resistant, and like its famous relative has glossy, deep green foliage.

'Sun Sprinkles' was only the fifth miniature rose ever to win AARS honors, and is the first to do so since 1993. The upright bush reaches twenty-four inches. Its high, pointed oval buds spiral open to form two-inch, petite, bright yellow blooms with moderate spicy fragrance. The dark green, glossy foliage is very disease-resistant. This variety was hybridized by John Walden for Bear Creek Gardens.

As the name implies, 'Marmalade Skies' produces brilliant orange-tangerine blooms. This floribunda, created also by the House of Meilland, has olive-green satiny foliage and clusters of five to eight blooms per stem. Its growth habit is compact—three feet by three feet—and it has good disease resistance.

If you prefer roses with strong fragrance, consider the new English Legend series of roses created by Harkness of England. Harkness roses have won many awards throughout the world with old-fashioned flowers and strong fragrance. They're available only by mail order from Heirloom Roses in Oregon. According to John Clements, owner of Heirloom Roses, this new series offers the rich fragrance and old-fashioned charm of antique roses with the virtues of modern breeding emphasizing disease resistance.

Shrub roses continue to grow in popularity. Romantica Roses, from the House of Meilland, are France's entry into an increasingly popular category. The Romantica Roses offer strong disease resistance and old-fashioned flowers on shrubs small enough to fit into urban gardens. However, I found the first wave of introductions sadly lacking in fragrance. This year, several new varieties are available and these have stronger fragrance. Among the newcomers are 'Francois Rabelais', with red-wine quartered flowers; 'Peter Mayle', with deep pink very fragrant flowers, and 'Michelangelo', a hybrid tea with lemon-yellow flowers and a slight citrus scent. This variety is a tall grower and produces very long stems. 'Carefree Sunshine' is another introduction by Meilland. This shrub rose is also a large plant and produces light yellow flowers on arching canes.

2002

For 2002, here are some of the exciting new introductions.

'Mellow Yellow'—I've had the opportunity to grow this rose in my own garden and it has captured my heart. This is a remarkable hybrid tea rose because it produces quantities of vivid yellow roses that retain their color, even in summer's heat. The plant has glossy green leaves with excellent disease resistance. An upright grower with moderate spread, it fits well into any landscape. This is an undemanding rose that even beginners will enjoy growing.

'Marilyn Monroe'—When Tom Carruth, the breeder of this new hybrid tea, read that the legendary actress Marilyn Monroe loved apricot colors, he contacted her foundation and obtained permission to name this beauty after the remarkable woman. Voluptuous, creamy apricot flowers with green wash last well in warm climates. The plant is strong, vigorous, and disease-free. Fragrance is a slight citrus.

'Outta the Blue'—This is another rose I've grown. I'm captivated by the old-fashioned-looking quartered blossoms, in fascinating hues of bluish magenta spiked with yellow. At times, the colors become more wine in hue. Its outstanding feature is fragrance—intense clove and rose—all the more remarkable because the plant has excellent disease resistance.

This is a free-flowering, very vigorous shrub and can easily grow to five feet or more.

'Crowd Pleaser'—Another strikingly colored rose—cerise pink with a white reverse—this hybrid tea is a "sport," a naturally occurring variation of an existing variety named 'Lynn Anderson'. Rosarian Chris Greenwood spotted the newcomer in his Glendora garden, and thanks to Tom Carruth and Weeks roses, now other rose enthusiasts can enjoy this elegant beauty in their own gardens.

'Electric Blanket'—Accomplishing what a groundcover rose is supposed to, this very clean, disease-free plant puts out masses of coral pink flowers to blanket the ground.

Also new in 2002 were two noteworthy Climbing Roses, 'Spice So Nice' and 'What A Peach'. 'Spice So Nice' is the only soft apricot-peach-colored climbing rose. It produces very fragrant flowers in large clusters and the plant has impeccably clean foliage.

'What A Peach' is supposed to be a small shrub, but in a warm climate behaves like a miniature climbing rose. Apricot colored ruffled flowers, small in size and large in quantity, appear regularly from spring through winter.

There were only two AARS winners for 2002, 'Love and Peace' and 'Starry Night'. 'Love and Peace' is a hybrid tea with exhibition-form flowers in soft yellow splashed with pink. It is heavily petalled, so does not perform at its best in places where cool evenings can keep the flowers from fully opening. However, 'Starry Night' blooms brilliantly, producing huge clusters of single, five petalled blossoms of pure white, accented with showy gold stamens. A shrub rose, it blooms heavily throughout the year, and is disease free. Alas, it lacks fragrance.

If you're a fan of the David Austin English roses, you'll be pleased with the release in the U.S. of eight new varieties. Prized for their old-fashioned flowers and strong fragrance, the David Austin roses also have a reputation for growing very large in warm climates. 'England's Rose' is a dainty, delicate rose of soft apricot that stays under four feet. This charming rose was selected by the Royal National Rose Society to commemorate the life and work of Diana, Princess of Wales.

'Miss Alice' is another dainty rose that stays at about three feet. Large soft pink flowers perfume a border with old rose fragrance. Another variety with very large flowers is 'Charles Darwin'. Rounded yellow flowers open to shallow cup forms and exude floral tea or lemon fragrance.

2003

Some days, it looks like smoky orange. Other days it resembles milk cocoa. And at times the flowers look cinnamon brown with tinges of rust orange. Whatever the day, it's a sensational rose. This unusual floribunda named 'Hot Cocoa' is one of the four AARS selections for 2003.

I can attest to the worth of 'Hot Cocoa' because I had the opportunity to trial it in my own garden for the past year. It's remarkable because it flowers very freely and is also very disease-resistant since its thick, glossy leaves aren't affected by mildew and rust. The flowers are almost nonstop. Some varieties tend to "crop"—produce their flowers in one batch and then gather strength to bloom again in eight to ten weeks. Not 'Hot Cocoa'. Each plant is rarely without some stage of flower—buds to fully opened—from spring through late fall.

The long-stemmed clusters consist of four-inch flowers with very unusual colors that have to be seen to be believed. This variety holds color and substance even in heat.

"It's a color you either love or hate and fortunately most people love it," said Tom Carruth, who created this sensational rose. During his illustrious rose breeding career, he has created an impressive number of AARS winners including 'Fourth of July', a climbing rose of vibrant colors. Carruth created this award-winning rose in 1993 (it takes ten years for a new rose to be developed, tested, and prepared for marketing). He said he knew he had something really outstanding just by looking at the foliage before the young seedling had even produced its first flower. "When I saw the first bloom, I thought it was most novel," he recalled. "The color is quite indescribable."

The other three AARS roses were 'Whisper', a white hybrid tea, 'Eureka', a yellow, apricot, gold colored floribunda, and 'Cherry Parfait', a grandiflora that produces white flowers, each with a broad edge of red.

2004

The AARS winners for 2004 are in.

'Day Breaker' is a floribunda with quantities of delicately colored ruffled flowers in hues of yellow blending to light pink and apricot. Its fragrance is moderate. The plant is bushy and medium-height, with glossy dark green leaves that have good disease resistance.

'Honey Perfume' is a floribunda that offers clusters of large apricot-yellow flowers with enticing spicy fragrance on a plant that's very resistant to rust and powdery mildew. Its growth habit is bushy.

'Memorial Day' is a lovely hybrid tea with long cutting stems—all the better to enjoy the remarkable clear pink flowers with a hint of lavender. Each flower can perfume a room with its strong damask rose fragrance. The plant is vigorous, tall, and easy to grow, as the rich green leaves have very good disease resistance.

"Pesto and Roses"
companion plants

WHEN I PLANTED MY FIRST ROSE BUSHES IN 1983, various experts advised me never to mix other plants with them. At that time, conventional wisdom, especially among people growing roses for trophies and blue ribbons, was that no other plant should mar the rose's ability to absorb all the fertilizer and water it needed to produce those show-stopping marvelous flowers.

After several years of enjoying rows of roses, I decided to break out of the pattern and mix and match. After all, my real interest was in creating a garden; not just collecting an assortment of rose bushes. Happily, conventional wisdom has warmed to the fact that roses and many other plants do indeed mix and mingle freely. There are many benefits to growing an assortment of plants, instead of just a monoculture.

Clair Martin, rose curator at the Huntington Botanical Gardens, likes to include an assortment of perennial plants, herbs, and some vegetables in his rose garden in Pasadena. "I like lemon-scented thyme as a groundcover because it gives off such a lovely scent when I walk on it," he says. "I also like to include borders of parsley or opal basil so I can harvest for my table as well as my vases. I can have pesto and roses," he adds with a smile.

Sometimes Martin includes clusters of oak leaf lettuces that form low mounded edging for borders. In my garden, I've experimented with Rainbow Swiss chard and like the effect of its yellow or red stalks, topped with deep green leaves. It's especially showy in front of my yellow floribunda 'Easy Going'.

Including companion plants into a rose bed or garden lessens the likelihood of damage from invading insect pests, especially with companion plants that attract the "good" bugs. I appreciate the fragrance from sweet alyssum flowers. The hover flies that feed on their nectar and pollen also eat the bad bugs feeding on my roses.

Another benefit to including companion plants is that they camouflage the sometimes unsightly "bare leg" syndrome that can happen to hybrid teas. As they grow, leaves and flowers concentrate at the mid to upper section of the bush.

When selecting companion plantings for roses, be sure to pick out plants with similar horticultural requirements. This way, when you feed and water the roses, you don't have to provide different care for the plants gracefully growing at their bases.

There's a wide selection of plants that will complement roses. Choices include true geraniums that are low-growing, mounding perennials with gray foliage and small flowers, scented-leaf geraniums, asters, snow-in-summer, baby-blue-eyes, cosmos, lavender, lemon balm, marigolds, nasturtiums, irises, violas, and violets. Some of these may reseed freely and spread where you don't want them, but judicious weeding will keep problems to a minimum. Also be sure to keep the base of roses free from plant growth. Sunlight stimulates new cane production.

If you run out of room for full-size rose bushes, you can tuck miniature roses in front of their larger relatives. I like to use the proportionately smaller flowers in arrangements for tiny vases. If you decide to border your roses with miniatures, be sure to tuck in some companion plants for a variety of color and flowers.

I stopped using pesticides and other types of toxic chemicals in my garden years ago. I prefer to let the beneficial insects that my garden attracts keep the insect invaders in check. I can also harvest my basil, nasturtium flowers (they add a slightly spicy flavor to salads), and Swiss chard without fear of poisoning my guests or myself.

Petals from hybrid tea roses can be used in tea sandwiches. Be sure no chemical sprays have been used on the roses, and trim off the white ends before garnishing each tea sandwich with one or two petals.

The Birth of a Rose

PATIENTLY PURSUING HIS QUEST to create the perfect rose, hybridizer Tom Carruth has come close to realizing his dream with his recent superb rose aptly named 'Scentimental'. It won the coveted AARS award in 1997 and was the first striped rose to do so. Roses are judged in trial gardens nationwide for a two-year period. Only the best of the best win this coveted designation.

'Scentimental' is a floribunda that can grow more than four feet in warm climates. It features unusual flowers with burgundy and cream striped petals and very sweet spice fragrance. 'Scentimental' evokes the look and scent of the striped hybrid roses of the 1800s. In addition to the unusual patterning of the flowers (no two are alike), one of its best virtues is that 'Scentimental' is virtually disease-free. It is a breakthrough rose because roses that have the genes for fragrance like lavender varieties can also be prone to diseases like mildew and rust. The latter is genetically linked to lavender roses, which are prone to these troublesome fungal diseases.

Carruth spent nine years developing and evaluating 'Scentimental' before selecting it for AARS consideration. Its parents are 'Playboy' and 'Peppermint Twist'. "I'm always searching for the novel and new," says the gifted rose man. "I'm particularly fascinated with the different petal patterns in striped roses."

Each year, Carruth evaluates his breeding goals and selects the parent plants from the many thousands of rose varieties already in existence. He uses eight hundred mature roses, consisting of 120 varieties, planted in seven-gallon containers that grow in controlled conditions. When the parent plants bloom in March, the anthers (male portion of the flower) are removed so that the roses can't pollinate themselves. Instead, Carruth and a small crew of helpers hand-pollinate each of 24,000 flowers in March and another 24,000 at the second bloom cycle in July. They tag the pollinated flowers with identification numbers and Carruth patiently waits for seed hips to ripen over the summer.

Each October, 200,000 seeds are harvested and planted in eight specially constructed raised beds. Although not all germinate, Carruth has a large number of babies to nurture and evaluate.

Then the evaluation process begins as Carruth personally inspects each bed and eliminates the seedlings that don't meet his criteria. In the first year, he eliminates all but one thousand. When they are one year old, they are carefully removed from the beds, and budded to rootstock to create ten plants of each variety. The young plants are shipped to the Weeks growing fields in Wasco, California, where the evaluation process continues for another two years. Carruth eliminates all but fifty varieties at the end of the first year of field testing, and the following year selects the twenty best varieties. Of those twenty, ten are entered in the AARS trials.

'Scentimental' was first created in 1988, and Carruth knew he had developed an outstanding rose. "From the time it emerged in the planting bed, it stood out from all the thousands of seedlings surrounding it," he recalls. "I didn't know at that time that it would be an award-winner, but I knew right away that it was a very high-quality rose."

Although Carruth has been breeding roses for more than two decades and has created roses that have earned acclaim, 'Scentimental' is his first AARS winner. It wasn't his last. More AARS winners are 'Betty Boop', 'Cl. Fourth of July', also a striped rose, 'Hot Cocoa', and 'Memorial Day'.

If there is a gene for gardening, Carruth may well have inherited it because he recalls being influenced by both his grandmothers, who loved to garden. He often helped them tend their gardens while growing up in Texas. Carruth pursued his passion for horticulture at Texas A&M University, where he obtained both bachelor's and master's degrees in horticulture. Involved in the rose industry since 1975, he gained on-the-job experience from breeders William Warriner and Jack Christensen (of the former Armstrong Nurseries in California). With Christensen, Carruth bred 'Crystalline', a pure white hybrid tea rose rated as the second best exhibition rose in the U.S. When Armstrong merged with Jackson & Perkins in 1987, Carruth joined Weeks Roses and began to develop his own breeding program.

Always in quest of the perfect rose, Carruth seeks to create a rose that he defines as "fragrant, completely clean, vigorous, has excellent flower form with pleasing color and finish, lots of blooms, quick to repeat, and very hardy." But he agrees that this perfect rose has not yet been achieved, and may never be. Even 'Scentimental', as excellent as it is, may have detractors if people don't like striping in roses. Those who do love 'Scentimental' may wish that the rose blooms remained longer. The buds open and stay on the plant for just a few days, unlike some varieties that can last up to a week. "It's a rose that people have strong opinions about—either they love it or they hate it," Carruth says.

So, Carruth remains on his mission to create the perfect rose even though he knows it's a lifetime quest. "Besides, if I did create the perfect rose, I'd be out of a job," he says with a laugh.

Roses for Mother's Day

MOTHER'S DAY IS A NATURAL TIME to show mothers how much we love and appreciate them. Roses are the timeless symbol of love and a gift that Mom is certain to enjoy. And what a nice, personal gesture an elegant bouquet of roses from your very own garden can be. But perhaps your rose bushes are between flower cycles or you don't have enough for a full bouquet. Your next thought might be to buy some from your local florist. Have you ever wondered why the rose varieties you love to grow are never for sale in florist stores?

The reason is that professional rose breeders create two distinct types of roses, depending on their destinations. Garden roses are bred with characteristics that make them suitable for landscape displays in garden settings. Florist roses, or cut roses, are created to serve completely different purposes. I spoke with Keith Zary, rose hybridizer for Jackson & Perkins, to find out what really makes garden roses different from cut roses. Zary, who breeds roses for both markets, says, "It's very rare for a garden rose to be used in commercial cut rose production. Rose plants used in the cut rose industry are really regarded as flower factories. They produce six or seven crops every year, resulting in thirty to sixty stems and blooms each year. After seven years, the plants are replaced with new ones."

Compare this with garden roses that can live and thrive for a century or more. Even though we can enjoy roses almost year-round, our garden varieties produce four or five cycles of bloom.

Cut rose growers usually want hybrid teas that produce one elegant bloom per long

stem. They shun varieties that produce side buds because of the cost of manual labor to disbud each cluster. Garden hybrid tea stems are considered long if they are fourteen to eighteen inches. Cut roses must have stem lengths at least twenty-two to thirty inches to be considered long. Petal quality also varies. "Garden roses are more ephemeral," Zary says. "Petals can drop in three to five days. But cut roses have to last from the time they're harvested, transported maybe fifteen thousand miles, then prepared for sale. And the consumer expects them to last at least a week. To achieve this, we have to breed roses with very thick petals that look and feel like plastic or cardboard."

Rose breeders can experiment with novel colors for roses destined for landscapes. But when it comes to roses for bouquets, the all-out favorite pick is red, followed by yellow, white, and pink. But don't expect those elegant red beauties to emit perfume. "There's not as much fragrance in cut roses as in garden roses because commercial rose growers prefer other characteristics that make them flourish under greenhouse conditions," Zary explains.

> Most cut roses originate in greenhouses in Latin America.

Cut roses are rarely sold by varietal name. Instead, select the color that you know will please. If you decide to select a rose plant for Mom, you might want to consider one of Zary's following recommendations. Many rose fanciers want an outstanding fragrant red hybrid tea. The old favorite, 'Mister Lincoln', is still a top seller because of its strong fragrance even though more recent red roses lack its aroma, but have improved color and growth characteristics. So Zary adds the following to his red recommendations:

'Opening Night'
'Olympiad'
'Veteran's Honor'
You can also consider the red rose, 'Ingrid Bergman', included among the world's top ten roses.

Zary also recommends the following pink hybrid tea varieties:

'New Zealand'
'Secret'
'Sheer Bliss'
'Pristine'
'Fragrant Memory'

The December Roses

I NEVER MET A ROSE I DIDN'T LIKE. This becomes a great problem when I want to try new varieties, because there just isn't any more room in my garden unless I take something out. I'm always faced with this dreadful dilemma every November and December, when the avalanche of rose catalogues overwhelms me.

My desk is littered with colorful catalogues from rose companies around the nation. The Internet adds to my predicament, for now I can log on to English and French nurseries with just the tap of a few computer keys and discover even more varieties that are just asking to live in my garden.

So at the time of year when I'm mindful of the holiday spirit that inspires us to strive for peace on earth and goodwill to all, I must harden my heart, steel my resolve, and decide the fate of innocent plants.

This isn't as ruthless as it may seem. In some parts of the nation, Mother Nature performs the task of culling out weak or diseased plants through the liberal application of freezing temperatures, snow, and ice. However, in warmer regions, gardeners need to be vigilant in culling the weak or poor performers. Early December is a good time for this task.

I study each rose plant carefully. Are there any in the garden that are struggling to flower with just one or two canes? I have a few like this. 'Paradise', with its sweet fragrance and two-toned flowers, is a plant that I keep hoping will send out new canes to supplement the existing two thick and gnarly ones. This has gone on for three years with no improvement, so I must consign 'Paradise' to the heavenly reward that awaits exhausted rose bushes. A healthy hybrid tea should have at least three or four canes. Shrubs, floribundas, and grandifloras often have more. There's no point in nursing a sickly rose bush when that valuable space can be put to better use by a vigorous newcomer.

I also look for flower power. Not all roses bloom with equal profusion. I want lots of flowers to reward the efforts I expend on tending roses. Those "stingy bloomers" that fail to produce more than six or seven in a cycle must make way for more floriferous varieties. So out comes 'Mister Lincoln', which only produces seven or eight roses in each bloom cycle. I really have to summon all my willpower for this because the heady perfume makes 'Mister Lincoln' among my favorites.

A note of caution here: it can take rose bushes at least two or three years to mature to their full flower production. Resist the temptation to rip out last year's plant because it failed to live up to your expectations. Climbing roses especially need to take their time in developing root systems before they start to flower in great quantities.

Also take note of colors and forms. For a while, I was fascinated with orange roses. But over time, I filled my garden with shades of pink and lavender. 'Voodoo', with its intense orange hues is now out of place next to the pink 'Tiffany' and the pale pink 'Secret'. 'Voodoo' must go.

Sometimes a rose is too exuberant. I love the David Austin English roses in my garden, but some English roses explode in warm sunshine. 'Brother Cadfael' is an example of an Austin rose that's just too happy in Southern California. Canes in excess of twelve feet consume far more than the plant's allotted space. So, out comes 'Brother Cadfael' as it tries to smother its closest neighbors.

When the bushes are still relatively young and healthy, I try to find good homes for them in other people's gardens. 'Brother Cadfael' will be transplanted in a yard where it can grow along a fence and throw as many long canes as it likes. Sometimes culling roses can have a happy ending when it means sharing something beautiful with a friend—especially if it includes visiting privileges!

In Search of
Rose Cultivars

DO YOU HAVE A FAVORITE ROSE from years ago that you wish you could find today? You're not alone. Many people have fond memories of a certain rose that grew in Grandma's garden. But as new roses are created, older varieties that don't sell quickly can be hard to find at local nurseries.

Alberta Terrazas, of Pico Rivera, wrote to me to ask where she could find a cherished red rose, 'Papa Meilland', that she bought twenty years ago. This very fragrant, dark red hybrid rose is still blooming heartily for her, and she would like to add another to her garden. Fortunately, there is a publication that specializes in identifying where rose varieties can be purchased. Called Combined Rose List, it's favored by rosarians who search out unusual or older rose cultivars. The extensive compendium is compiled and edited by Beverly R. Dobson and Peter Schneider, and has been published annually since 1980. Revised each year, this respected publication lists all roses now in commerce—some 11,500 varieties, from the newest hybrid teas to the most ancient species roses. If a nursery or mail order firm in North America as well as selected international nurseries sells the variety, this paperback book lists it.

I looked up 'Papa Meilland' and found that it is still available in the U.S. through Meilland-Star, the American wholesale company for Meilland Roses of France where this rose was created in 1963. Local nurseries can obtain this award-winning rose, which has the distinction of being named one of the world's favorite roses in 1988. More international nurseries sell this cultivar than American nurseries, but fortunately, it is still obtainable.

The sad fact in the world of rose sales is that if a variety isn't in demand, it is quickly replaced by the newer varieties. But just because a cultivar was created decades ago doesn't mean that it's not garden worthy. For example, 'King's Ransom', a brilliant yellow fragrant hybrid tea created in 1962 by Swim was an AARS winner that year. This fragrant rose is still cherished in many gardens, although a little hard to find now. (Weeks Roses is still a prime source).

Not all roses are that easy to get. One of my favorites, 'Gardens of the World', has occupied a prominent place in my garden since 1993, when it was introduced and sold through Jackson & Perkins. Now, only one nursery in the world sells it—and it's located in India. Just knowing that means I'm going to retain this hybrid tea for a long while.

Combined Rose List is approximately $20.00 plus shipping. For details, contact Peter Schneider, P.O. Box 677, Mantua, Ohio 44255.

During the Middle Ages, roses were used for medicine more than for decorative reasons. Rose vinegar was thought to relieve the pain of headaches.

Celebrity Roses

WHEN PAUL MCCARTNEY was about to celebrate his fiftieth birthday, his family wanted to honor the famous singer in a very special way. They contacted the House of Meilland, international rose hybridizers whose famous roses include the classic 'Peace'. Thus, in 1996 'The McCartney Rose' was born, a hybrid tea with fragrant deep rosy pink flowers.

Rose companies are well aware that even a so-so rose can become a hot seller if it has the right name. An example is the white hybrid tea 'John F. Kennedy' that is still cherished in many gardens today because of the tragic death of the late president. Similarly, 'Diana, Princess of Wales' honors one of the most celebrated women of the twentieth century.

There are dozens of roses named for celebrities, most often in the entertainment industry, although other prominent people have roses named in their honor. 'Billy Graham' is a hybrid tea with long pointed pink buds named in honor of the renowned reverend Billy Graham. Jackson & Perkins introduced it several years ago. "We wanted to honor a man who is such a widely admired and respected individual," explained William Ihle, vice president of corporate relations. "We sent samples of different new rose varieties to the Grahams so they could choose the rose themselves. Ruth Graham likes to garden and she made the selection."

When naming a rose, the process begins with choosing a name and then reserving it with the American Rose Society, which registers all new roses. If a name already has been reserved, it cannot be used again as long as the rose is still commercially sold. If the name involves a person, that person, or the person's estate, must give permission for use of the name. Rose companies approach celebrities in about half the cases, but celebrities also approach companies when they want a rose named in their honor.

"Sometimes celebrities don't want a rose named for them and will turn down the request," says Tom Carruth, who created roses that were named in honor of George Burns and Gracie Allen. The two floribundas were introduced in 1998. "George Burns personally selected the rose named for his late wife," Carruth says. "He selected it because he said it made him feel good when he looked at it."

'Gracie Allen' is white in bud stage and opens to reveal a pink heart that intensifies as it unfurls. The rose named for the late comedian Burns is flashy with yellow, red, and white stripes.

In all cases, the hybridizers try to match the celebrity with a rose that has some trait or characteristic in keeping with the person. One of the most cited examples is the coppery orange-red hybrid tea named for singer Dolly Parton. This rose produces very large, voluptuous flowers that are buxom as buds as well as in full bloom.

Singer Lynn Anderson has a hybrid tea named for her. The flowers are cream with a deep pink edging and the plant performs at its best in warm southern climates.

Other celebrity roses include 'Barbra Streisand', a beautiful purple hybrid tea with exceptional fragrance; 'Lucille Ball', a hybrid tea with carrot-orange flowers; 'Ingrid Bergman', a dark red hybrid tea with exquisitely formed flowers; 'Bing Crosby', a vibrant orange hybrid tea; 'Chris Evert', a hybrid tea with melon-orange flowers brushed with red; 'Whoopi', a deep red miniature; 'Cary Grant', a hybrid tea producing orange flowers blended with copper; 'Audrey Hepburn', a blush pink hybrid tea; 'Bob Hope', a bright red hybrid tea; and 'Elizabeth Taylor', a vibrant hot pink hybrid tea.

Try drying fresh rose blooms in silica gel.

Put fresh blossoms in a small box and add enough silica gel to cover. The gel will remove water from the petals, which will dry in two to four days. Use in potpourri or decorations.

make room for the
New European Roses

C HOOSING NEW ROSE VARIETIES is getting harder and harder as more and more varieties are created. Contending for our garden space are some newcomers from Europe. Two long-established and respected rose firms in France and Denmark are creating and selling series of roses to try to simplify selection. Instead of trying to remember the name of a specific variety you saw and admired, instead you can ask for a specific type of rose that has been created for landscape display.

From France come the Generosa series, developed by one of the oldest French nurseries, Roseraie Guillot. The 170-year-old company is best known for developing the first hybrid tea, 'La France', in 1867 and the first polyantha, 'Parqurette', in 1875. Since then, the firm has introduced more than two hundred new roses and now offers the Generosa series of shrub roses featuring very fragrant flowers with old rose form. Initial reports of the French response to the David Austin English roses are that they take less garden space than most Austin varieties, offer equal or stronger fragrance, and have good disease resistance.

When Jean-Pierre Guillot spoke at the Huntington Botanical Gardens in San Marino, California, he explained how his company developed the Generosa series with an enticing slide display. Although three varieties are available now, more will be introduced over the next few years. Rose curator Clair Martin, author of *One Hundred English Roses for the American Garden*, is a fan of the Generosa roses for their growth habits, flower form, color, and disease resistance.

The three varieties widely available are: 'Claudia Cardinale', an upright shrub producing quartered bright yellow flowers that finish as coppery red; 'Martine Guillot', a shrub with arching canes and cream colored buds that open as deeply cupped flowers blushed with soft apricot, and with an unusual gardenia-like fragrance; and 'Sonia Rykiel', which produces coral pink flowers with quartered form and very strong perfume.

From Poulsen Roses of Denmark, the 125-year-old company that first created the floribunda rose, comes the new Towne & Country series of shrub roses created specifically for landscapes. Bred and grown on their own roots, this series consists of twenty-six different varieties, ranging from spreading ground covers to four-foot shrubs. All have the same characteristics as masses of small flowers that don't require deadheading. They are extremely disease-resistant, and many are equally at home in the ground or in containers. Easy to grow because they only need shaping every year or two, these Towne & Country roses are ideal for people who love roses but don't have a lot of time to take care of them. Some of the varieties look like wild roses and emit a delectable honey fragrance. Others resemble compact floribundas, but with more massed blooms. They are very popular in Europe where they have won numerous awards and can be seen in public and private landscapes. Now, they are available at local nurseries, especially those that feature roses.

In ancient Rome, roses symbolized life, death, and eternal life. Romans revered and used roses so much that a special day, Rosalia, was set aside on May 23 for feasts celebrating roses.

conclusion

Enjoying Your Roses

ROSES BRING SMILES TO LIPS, sparkles to eyes, and delight to hearts. No matter how stressful my day, I always feel better when I visit my roses. Yes, I stop and smell the roses—and caress a lovely bloom, murmur words of praise to a graceful bush, and in general, experience the beauty of life. If you want to bring a smile to someone, present the person with a rose. Man or woman, young or old, each will respond with a smile of delight.

I like to experience my roses indoors as well and gather blossoms for bouquets. I also like to cut an especially plump and pretty rose flower and float it in a crystal bowl on my dining room table.

There are other ways to enjoy your roses. You can gather freshly opened flowers, carefully remove the petals, and serve them as a garnish on tea sandwiches. Be sure you haven't used any chemical or toxic sprays if you intend to consume them. Or you may prefer to scatter rose petals on plates as aesthetic garnishes. You can also add a rosy hint of mystery to sugar if you add clean, dry petals to a covered sugar bowl and let the oil permeate the sugar.

Try a rose soak for a luxurious experience. When Brenee Brown, a skilled therapist at Spa Gaucin, located in the St. Regis Monarch Beach Resort in California, relaxes in the pri-

vacy of her own home, she enjoys a rose bath. She cuts fragrant rose flowers when they are fully opened, carefully separates the petals, then adds them to hot bath water. The secret is to add the petals to hot water one-half hour before you want to soak. This time frame allows the rose oils to perfume the air and permeate the bath water, which should be cool enough for a pleasant soak. Light a rose-scented candle, and enjoy a serenely rosy retreat.

A good plan for a garden includes a bench or chair where you can sit surrounded by your roses. Don't fuss over chores left undone. Relax, watch the buds unfurl, see the leaves shimmer in the breeze, enjoy the graceful ballet of bees gathering pollen. If you take this time, the beauty inherent in roses will touch and transform your heart.

Simple Rose Care Schedule

Warm Climates
Regions that usually don't have frost

January–February
Prune existing rose bushes and remove old leaves.
Plant new bare-root roses.
Water as needed, according to rainfall and soil type.
Clean up old leaves and debris from garden and apply new mulch.
Sharpen pruning shears and clean other tools.

March–April
Plant roses from containers while rose selection is still the best for the year.
Fertilize when new growth is two inches or longer.
Watch for insect attacks. If severe, spray bushes with water, insecticidal soap, or similar
    non-toxic product.
Gather rose blossoms from mature plants only. Don't collect bouquets from young
    plants, for they need all their leaves to feed root systems.

May–June
Deadhead (remove spent blossoms) as needed.
Fertilize rose bushes after their first flush of bloom.
Watch for insect attacks.
Water as needed. Deeply soak each bush.
Visit a public rose garden if you'd like to learn about different varieties.
In humid climates, watch for blackspot and apply appropriate remedy.

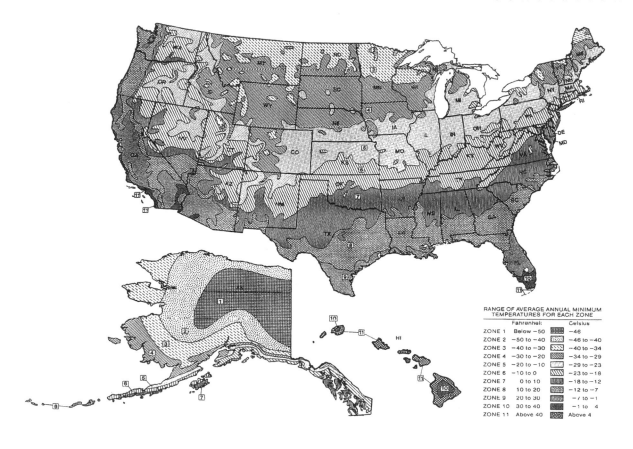

U.S.D.A. Plant Hardiness Zone Map

July–August

Continue to deadhead or gather flowers for bouquets.

Shape bushes as needed to retain attractive shape. If roses are taller than you can
  reach, cut their growth accordingly.

Add more mulch as needed.

Water as needed. Deeply soak each bush.

Continue to protect from insect attack. Spider mites are especially active in summer.

Reduce or stop fertilizing. Roses need this rest during hot summer months.

Remove weeds from around rose plants.

September–October

When temperatures cool, add the last fertilizer for the year if you want late season
  roses.

Water as needed.

Continue to deadhead or gather blooms.

November–December
Analyze your garden and decide if any rose bushes don't perform well. Dig up and
    remove any weak or undesirable bushes.
Study your garden to determine which new varieties you'd like to include.
Sharpen your pruning shears and prepare other tools for annual pruning.
In December, shop for bare-root roses in nurseries or order from catalogues.
Enjoy some time off while your garden rests.

Cold Climates
Frost and snow regions

January–February
Roses continue to slumber under a blanket of snow. If there hasn't been much cover in
    your area, be sure there's plenty of loose material covering your rose bushes for pro-
    tection.
Study rose catalogues and dream of spring.
Sharpen pruning shears and clean other tools.

March–April
When spring thaw ends, uncover rose bushes gradually to acclimatize them to tempera-
    ture change.
Prune back all dead or black wood.
Prune bushes to shape.
Plant bare-root bushes when ground is soft enough to dig (as late as May depending on
    your region).
When new growth is at least two inches long, fertilize.
Clean out old leaves and debris, then mulch.
Soak rose bushes if rainfall is scarce.

May–June
On mature plants, cut roses for bouquets as desired. Young plants need all their flowers
    and leaves to feed developing root systems.
Fertilize after the first flush of bloom.
Water deeply as needed if rains are lacking.
Deadhead as needed.
Visit a public rose garden to view more rose varieties.
Watch for signs of blackspot and treat accordingly.
Keep weeds away from rose bushes.
Watch for insect attacks and treat accordingly.

July–August
Apply the last fertilizer for the year.
Continue to check for water, if needed.
Deadhead or cut blossoms for bouquets.

September–October
Prepare roses for winter by withholding fertilizer.
Continue to deadhead as needed.

November–December
Prepare roses for winter protection by trimming back only if bushes won't fit into commercial rose cones.
Wait for two weeks after frost season starts before covering and protecting for winter.
Read rose books and plan for a new year.
Enjoy time off while your garden rests.

Sources

NURSERIES AND GARDEN CENTERS usually offer several hundred rose varieties. Specialty mail order nurseries often provide a larger selection. The following are among the leading nurseries that sell through catalogues or the Internet.

Modern Roses

Edmunds' Roses
6235 S.W. Kahle Road
Wilsonville, OR 97070
888-481-7673
Fax: 503-682-1275
Web site: www.edmundsroses.com

Jackson & Perkins
1 Rose Lane
P.O. Box 1028
Medford, OR 97501
800-292-4769
Fax: 800-242-0329
Web site: www.jacksonandperkins.com

Lowe's Roses
6 Sheffield Road
Nashua, NH 03063
603-888-2214
Web site: www.loweroses.com

Wayside Gardens
1 Garden Lane
Hodges, SC 29695
800-845-1124
Web site: www.waysidegardens.com

Syl Arena Roses
1041 Paso Robles Street
Paso Robles, CA 93446
888-466-7434
Fax: 888-347-5580
Web site: www.arenaroses.com

Antique and Similar Roses

Antique Rose Emporium
9300 Lueckemeyer Road
Brenham, TX 77833
800-441-0002
Fax: 409-836-9051
Web site: www.weAREroses.com

David Austin Roses Limited
15059 Highway 64 West
Tyler, TX 75704
800-328-8893
Fax: 903-526-1900
Web site: www.davidaustinroses.com

Heirloom Old Garden Roses
24062 N.E. Riverside Drive
St. Paul, OR 97137
503-538-1576
Fax: 503-538-5902

Miniature Roses

Nor'East Miniature Roses
P.O. Box 307
Rowley, MA 01969
800-426-6485
Web site: www.noreast-miniroses.com

Sequoia Nursery
2519 East Noble Avenue
Visalia, CA 93292
559-732-0309
Web site: ww.miniatureroses.com/moore

Where to Learn More about Roses

Rose Societies exist in many cities throughout North America. Contact The American Rose Society to find one in your region.

The American Rose Society
P.O. Box 30,000
Shreveport, LA 71130
800-637-6534
Web site: www.ars.org

Public botanical gardens are also sources for gardening classes. Check with one closest to you for details.

Index